JEAN CRAIGHEAD GEORGE
One Day in the Tropical Rain Forest
ILLUSTRATED BY GARY ALLEN

Here's all the great literature in this grade level of *Celebrate Reading!*

NUMBER THE STARS
a novel by Lois Lowry

CLASS PRESIDENT
by Johanna Hurwitz

MR. MYSTERIOUS & COMPANY

MARY POPPINS
REVISED EDITION
P.L. TRAVERS

Flights of Fancy

Journeys of the Imagination

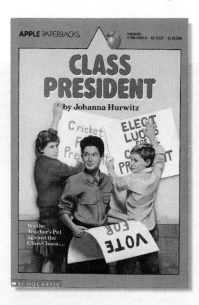

Class President
from the novel by Johanna Hurwitz
✻ Kentucky Bluegrass Award
✻ South Carolina Children's
Book Award

What a Wild Idea
by Louis Sabin

I'm Tipingee, She's Tipingee, We're Tipingee, Too
by Caroline Feller Bauer
✻ Christopher Award Author

The Voice of Africa in American Music
by Jim Haskins
✻ Coretta Scott King Award Author

The Third Gift
by Jan Carew
Illustrations by Leo and Diane Dillon

Ashanti to Zulu: African Traditions
from the book by Margaret Musgrove
Illustrations by Leo and Diane Dillon
✻ Boston Globe-Horn Book Award
✻ Caldecott Medal

Mary Poppins
from the novel by P. L. Travers
✻ Nene Award

Catwings
by Ursula K. Le Guin
✻ Children's Choice
✻ Irma Simonton Black Award

Featured Poet
Natalia Belting

Before Your Very Eyes
A World of Nature

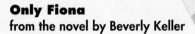

Featured Poets
Marilyn Singer
Byrd Baylor
George David Weiss
Bob Thiele

Many People, Many Voices

Stories of America

Featured Poets
Duke Redbird
Linh To Sinh My Bui

Within My Reach

The Important Things in Life

Handle with Care

Making a Difference

All About Sam
from the novel by Lois Lowry
✹ Mark Twain Award

Number the Stars
from the novel by Lois Lowry
✹ Newbery Medal
✹ ALA Notable Children's Book
✹ Teachers' Choice
✹ Notable Social Studies Trade Book

Jessi's Secret Language
from the novel by Ann M. Martin

Take a Walk in Their Shoes
from the biography by
Glennette Tilley Turner
✹ Notable Social Studies Trade Book

Dorothea Lange: Life Through the Camera
from the biography by
Milton Meltzer
✹ Boston Globe-Horn Book
Award Author

Featured Poets
Ouida Sebestyen
Danny Williams

Ask Me Again Tomorrow

Growing and Changing

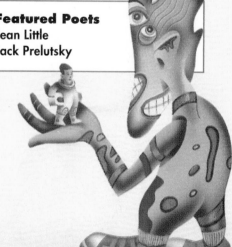

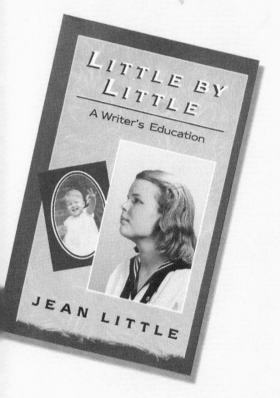

LITTLE BY LITTLE
A Writer's Education

JEAN LITTLE

B E F O R E
YOUR VERY EYES

A World of Nature

The Cover Story

Tom Bookwalter, the artist for the cover of *Before Your Very Eyes,* was particularly excited with this assignment: he is an avid outdoorsman who lives on a lake in a small Kansas town. His art technique for the cover reflects his reverence for nature. Each image you see is a black and white photograph that Mr. Bookwalter painstakingly painted by hand. He felt this was the best way to capture the brilliant colors of the birds, animals, and insects he chose to work with.

ISBN 0-673-80052-0

Acknowledgments appear on page 144.

5678910RRS999897969594

BEFORE
YOUR VERY EYES

A World of Nature

 ScottForesman

A Division of HarperCollinsPublishers

Contents

WONDERFUL NATURE

TOMORROW'S WORLD
GENRE STUDY

STUDENT RESOURCES

Count On Fiona

from *Only Fiona* by Beverly Keller

It's better never to be famous than to be famous for just a few days," Fiona Foster told her mother while they cleaned up after breakfast.

Mrs. Foster brushed off the place mats. "I wouldn't know."

"I was famous when we first moved here." Fiona stacked the dishes and saucers and cups and carried them over to the dishwasher. It was always interesting—and a little scary—to see how many breakable things she could carry in one trip. Her parents seemed to trust her to not make too wobbly a pile, but she could not help imagining the terrible and exciting mess there would be if things weren't balanced quite right.

"Anybody can be famous with other kids just by being new in town." Fiona set the cups and saucers and dishes on the counter beside her father. "But does it last? No! In a day or two, it's all over."

"There are drawbacks to being famous," her father observed.

"I didn't notice any." Fiona watched him stick the knives and forks and spoons into the dishwasher basket every which way.

"Truly famous people can't go anywhere without being pestered for autographs," he reminded her.

"I could live with it," Fiona said.

Mrs. Foster carried the syrup and margarine to the refrigerator. "Don't put the knives in the dishwasher with the points up," she reminded her husband, without even looking to see if that was what he was doing.

The house they'd lived in before had had no dishwasher. It had had only one bathroom, and a small, scrubby backyard. Six weeks had passed since they had moved out of that house, and Fiona still thought of it as home.

The house they lived in now had two stories, two bathrooms, and a yard with a big patio and plenty of room for a swing set. The only thing wrong with the new house was that it felt like a new house.

She knew there were very good reasons for moving from Kelsey, where she'd lived all her life, to Elvern.

"A job offer like this doesn't come every day," her mother had told her solemnly. "Elvern is ten times bigger than Kelsey, and Molberry's Department Store there is in a brand-new shopping mall, and your father

Even before she'd moved to Elvern, she had longed for a dog, or a cat, or even a rat—more than a brother or sister, in fact. Some of her friends in Kelsey had had brothers and sisters. Some had had pets. Fiona could not help noticing the difference: Animals didn't need diaper changing, or have tantrums, or try to grab all the good shades of crayons.

It was definitely a handicap to have parents who were allergic to dog hair, cat hair, and feathers—and who weren't too crazy about rats.

With her first allowance after moving to Elvern, Fiona had bought a dog dish. "Sweetheart," her mother had said patiently, but looking a little worried, "this is no way to try to pressure us into getting a dog."

"I know," Fiona had told her. "But a dog dish is a sensible thing to put outside in summer. People have birdbaths, but hardly anybody worries about dogs and cats out on the streets in hot weather."

So far, no dog or cat had dropped by for a drink, but a bee had dropped into the dish. Fiona had had a tense and scary time fishing it out of the dish and taking it to a safe place to dry off.

Since then, she'd left the dog dish empty when she wasn't around to watch it.

As Fiona was

will be manager of the entire optical department."

"It will be a real opportunity for your mother," Mr. Foster had told Fiona earnestly. "There's no future for a computer programmer in a town where the biggest business is Kelsey Lumber and Hardware. This way, she'll be in contact with up-and-coming firms that understand about computers."

Against all these good and serious reasons, what argument did Fiona have? Only "I don't want to go." She had said it a couple of times, just as solemnly and earnestly, but it had only set off a new round of sincere explanations from her parents. Finally she had given up, realizing they were going to move no matter what.

In the six weeks they'd lived in Elvern, Fiona had seen enough of it to realize it was a much handsomer town than Kelsey. Just a few blocks from Fiona's new house was a huge park. Its trees were so tall and leafy, they seemed to be whispering even when there was no breeze. There were acres of fine, close-trimmed grass, with gentle mounds you could roll down if you took a notion.

Molberry's Department Store was the biggest store Fiona had ever seen, set in the middle of a shopping mall that was nearly as dazzling as Disneyland. Molberry's Optical Department had brand-new carpeting and chairs and *four* glass-topped tables with mirrors where customers could sit and try on frames.

The only thing wrong with Elvern, Fiona thought, is that it feels like a new town, too.

"The hardest thing about leaving a place," she told her mother now, "is giving up your friends. I knew most of those kids in Kelsey so long, I couldn't even remember how I met them. The neat thing about friends like that is that you can just count on them. You know. Not for anything special. Just to be around." She started wiping down the counter. "You don't even care about being famous when you have friends to count on."

"You've made new friends since we moved here," her mother reminded her gently.

"Not to count on. Besides, they all live blocks away." Fiona set the sponge beside the sink. "To learn to live in a new place, you have to have a brother or a sister or a dog or a cat going through it with you, or friends you can count on."

No sooner had she gotten the last word out than Fiona realized she hadn't included parents among the things she could count on. Not only that, the things she *had* mentioned, like brothers and sisters, were mostly things parents provide. In one sentence, she thought, I insulted my mother and father in at least two different ways.

"I think it's my personality," she said hastily, to let them know she didn't blame them. "There's something about me that makes people take me for granted. Look at the kids I've met in Elvern. The only time Pauline comes looking for me is when she can't find Barbara. The only time Barbara comes over is when she's looking for Pauline. When Howard went to the beach, he left his dog with me because Spike gets carsick. Then he took Larry."

Mr. Foster glanced helplessly at Mrs. Foster.

Mrs. Foster put her arms around Fiona, getting a smear of syrup on her neck. "You're having a bad day, aren't you, love?"

"It's only morning," Fiona pointed out.

"Things are bound to get better," her father assured her. "It takes a while to settle in, but once you get used to Elvern, you'll be glad we moved here."

Fiona had a feeling that if she asked "Why?" or "When?" she would get no more-definite answers, so she only nodded. There was no point depressing her parents, and herself, any more than she had already.

As soon as the kitchen was tidied, she went out on the front porch.

It was a lovely, lazy Saturday morning, warm enough already for running through the sprinklers, if you had anybody to run through the sprinklers with. Fiona could imagine nothing more embarrassing than being seen running through a sprinkler all by yourself.

Across the street, a man was trimming his front hedge with electric clippers. Next door to him a woman was mowing her front lawn with an electric mower.

One thing about a nice neighborhood, Fiona thought, the people certainly take care of their yards. They certainly have the machinery to do it with, too.

At least the Fourth of July had been over for a week, so there was no need to go around tensed for stray firecracker explosions.

Fiona picked up her red dog dish and carried it down to the faucet under the living room window.

filling the dish, Barbara Lawson tromped up the walk, pushing her little brother, Oliver, in his stroller.

Almost eleven, Barbara was a few months older than Fiona, and half a head taller. Her hair was a darker brown than Fiona's, and cut shorter, and her eyes were a light brown flecked with bits of gold. She was square built but not bulky. Fiona could imagine her growing up to be a general, or maybe a wrestler. Barbara did not look like a person who backed down easily.

She was also the first genuine child grump Fiona had ever met. Back in Kelsey there were a few grownups who were generally known to be grumps—everybody avoided cutting across their front yards, or cut across on purpose just to get a reaction.

A child grump, though, was something Fiona had never run into before. She had known kids who were irritable now and then, but Barbara was just grumpy by nature, grumpy at everybody, and grumpy for no particular reason. Fiona couldn't help wondering whether Barbara had been born that way, or whether she had grown into it. She pictured a newborn Barbara, squalling in her cradle, glaring at the world.

If there was a naturally cranky strain running in Barbara's family, her little brother, Oliver, did not seem to have caught it.

Every time Fiona had seen him so far, he'd been in his stroller. Oliver seemed to take things as they came. He looked to be somewhere between one and two years old; Fiona had never bothered to ask, since he didn't do anything very interesting.

His hair was blond and soft and curly, his gaze was innocent and gentle, and he didn't talk, which made him almost as agreeable to be around as a dog.

As a matter of fact, Oliver seemed to have more in common with the average dog than with his sister. He took an interest in things that any human over the age of two generally overlooked. He peered at everything he passed in his stroller, and tried to smell and taste anything he got his hands on. He fussed hard, but not long, when his sister grabbed leaves or tree bark or old gum wrappers as he was about to eat them.

Barbara stomped up Fiona's walk now. Even when she was in a relatively good mood, Barbara tended to walk as if she were punishing the sidewalk on general principles.

"Nobody's home at Pauline's," she greeted Fiona. "I wonder where she went."

Fiona carried the dog dish up to the porch. What would happen, she wondered, if I just came right out and said, "Do you know you never come around here unless you're looking for Pauline?"

"Do you remember her saying anything about where she was going?" Barbara stood with her hands on the stroller handle, ready to take off the minute she knew where Pauline was.

Before Fiona could answer, she saw Howard Broyhill crossing the street with his dog, Spike.

Howard was barely ten, but taller than Barbara. His skin was the color of chocolate, and his hair was black and crisp and curly. Fiona had never seen him without Spike, who looked like a sheepdog mixed with an assortment of other breeds. Spike's back legs were longer than his front legs, so he walked rather like a bear. His hair was long, gray and white, and shaggy, even on his head—Fiona had never been able to get a good look at his eyes.

Howard patted Oliver on the head absently, as he would a dog, and told Fiona and Barbara, "My folks are taking me—"

Fiona set down the dog dish. "And you want me to watch Spike."

Howard looked surprised. "No. We won't be gone that long. My folks said I could bring a couple of friends. You guys want to come—without Oliver?"

Spike plopped his front right paw in the dog dish, sloshing water over the porch. Fiona barely noticed. This was the first time anyone in Elvern had asked her to go anywhere. "Yeah! Sure! Great!"

"Where?" Barbara asked.

"To the zoo."

Fiona's delight fizzed away like the bubbles from a soda that's been left out all day. The whole idea of zoos made her sad. "No, thanks."

"What's the matter?" Howard asked.

"I've been to the zoo." Fiona just wanted to go inside and be left alone to feel disappointed in private.

"There's some law against going twice?" Barbara wanted to know. Barbara often asked questions that were like statements.

Fiona suspected it was because they sounded grumpier that way.

"A minute ago you were all excited," Howard reminded Fiona.

"It's the animals," she explained.

"That's why you *go* to the zoo." Barbara spoke as if she were explaining to a visitor from another planet. "You *go* to look at the animals."

"Cooped up in cages?" Fiona could see she was upsetting Howard and Barbara, but she felt she owed it to the zoo animals to speak out.

"You want them walking the streets?" Barbara demanded. "Riding the bus? Shopping in the mall?"

Though Fiona was impressed that Barbara could fire three sentence-questions in a row, she was not even tempted to back down. "They should be where they can do what they feel like doing, and not just hang around being watched," she said firmly.

"Hey, they have a good time!" But Howard was beginning to sound as if he were trying to convince himself. "Didn't you ever see the bears beg for peanuts?"

"Would you sit up and grab your feet and rock back and forth for a crummy peanut?" Fiona asked.

"Okay. That's it. Forget it." Barbara whirled Oliver's stroller around. "Nobody can talk to her."

Fiona sat on her porch steps, watching Howard and Barbara walk away with Oliver. Spike followed them, sniffing at bugs and twigs, and catching his leash under his front leg.

Even knowing Barbara was a grump didn't make Fiona feel better. Here it is, barely after breakfast, she thought, and I've already insulted my parents and Barbara and Howard, the only person in this town who's ever invited me anyplace. And he came to my house first, not Barbara's.

The idea hit her, *whop!*, just like that.

"Hey!" She leaped to her feet and ran after Howard and Barbara.

They stopped while she caught up.

"You might as well leave Spike with me," she said, trying to sound casual and offhand.

"Great!" One neat thing about Howard, he didn't cherish a grudge. He handed Spike's leash to Fiona. "He'll be a lot happier with a person than with a chew toy." Howard bent to kiss the bit of wet black nose that showed through Spike's hair.

"We'll dump Oliver at my house first," Barbara told Howard, as if Fiona hadn't done anything noble or generous at all.

"You're sure you don't mind leaving him?" Howard asked.

"Do you think I'd go for a long ride with anybody who wears diapers?" Barbara started walking again, pushing the stroller.

And that was it. Not so much as "Wow, Fiona, what a big favor." Not even "You must really love dogs, Fiona."

As Howard caught up to her, Barbara asked, "Who else shall we get to come with us?"

"I don't know," Fiona heard him say. "Everybody else either isn't home or has something to do."

A person can be too offhand and casual, Fiona reflected.

She led Spike back to her house. It was only half a

block, but it took time. Since he walked with his face inches from the ground he noticed a lot of things the average person overlooks. Every few steps he stopped to sniff, and lick, and nudge things with his nose.

Fiona reached her front yard as her mother came out the door.

"Oh, Fiona." Mrs. Foster looked surprised. "You were just complaining about watching that dog."

Fiona didn't answer. The dog, she thought, is the only person so far this morning who hasn't told me I'm just having a bad day, or that nobody can talk to me.

Mrs. Foster hurried toward the station wagon. Your mother may make mistakes sometimes, like giving you slapdash comfort when you need serious sympathy, but there's no sense doing yourself out of a ride that could end with a stop for a banana split. Fiona went after her. "Where are you going?"

Mrs. Foster unlocked the door of the old blue station wagon. "Just to pick up some spray. We've got ants coming in under the kitchen sink."

Fiona pulled Spike back as he tried to crowd into the wagon. "You're going to spray them before you even find out what they plan to do?"

"Fiona, I am really not prepared to argue about ants' plans."

Fiona could see that her mother was in no mood to discuss the matter.

"You've probably never watched ants enough to think about them," Fiona said. "Ants are neat, when you get to know them."

Mrs. Foster slid into the car.

Spike planted his front paws on the hood, barking urgently.

Looking a little strained, Mrs. Foster waited for Fiona to haul Spike down on all fours. Then she put the key in the ignition. "Try to keep him quiet, honey. The last time he stayed here, he howled and yapped and drove us half crazy."

"But he settled down."

"He lay on his back on our porch with his legs stiff in the air. The neighbors probably thought we'd taken up taxidermy."

"Tax . . . like in taxes or taxis?"

"Taxidermy." Mrs. Foster turned the key. "Stuffing dead animals so they look almost alive. I guess you never saw the moose head on the wall of the sporting goods department at Kelsey Lumber and Hardware."

Fiona stood back from the car. "Mother! That is *gross!*"

"Indeed. So keep Spike quiet, and off his back." Mrs. Foster drove away.

The station wagon's paint had gone dull, and even the license plates were dented and old. In any other family where both parents earned money, Fiona thought, there would be two cars, or at least one that looked respectable.

"But that's the way my folks are." She led Spike

back up the porch steps and sat down. "My dad spends half his day fitting contact lenses, but he wears glasses. My mom works all day at her computer with *her* glasses sliding down her nose, so she has to shove them back every two minutes."

It occurred to her that Spike probably hadn't seen his own mother since he was a few weeks old. The idea made her so sad, she had to grumble a little just to keep from feeling more downcast.

"When your own mother doesn't even ask if you want to come to the store," she told Spike, "that shows how much she thinks of you. Sure, she'd say it was because certain dogs around here have a reputation for getting carsick. Sure, I wouldn't go— that would be like approving of ant spray. But she could have at least asked."

Spike slumped against Fiona so she had to brace herself.

"Sure, Barbara says nobody can talk to me," Fiona went on, "but what does everybody talk to me *about?* About animals locked up in zoos. About moose heads on walls. About murdering ants. I mean, these ants wander in under the sink, right? Were there any *Keep Out* signs to warn them? They're not planning to steal our TV, after all. Maybe they're looking for something to eat. Maybe they're *starving*. Since when is that a crime? Maybe they're just going to take a look around and then get out of there. But right away, *zap!*, they're massacred."

Spike twisted his head around to chew at imaginary fleas on his shoulder.

So long as she was resenting things, Fiona told him

about the time she got in trouble for accidentally scuffing her new patent-leather shoes. Then she told him how she got blamed when she was five for biting her cousin Ethel, even though Ethel had pinched her first.

Spike snored a soft, wet-sounding snore.

Fiona tied his leash to the porch rail and went into the house to try to reason with her father.

He was squatting beside the dishwasher, taking cleaners and detergents and scouring pads from the cabinet under the sink.

Gazing around the kitchen, Fiona said, "I see they haven't taken over or anything."

He took out a bottle of plant fertilizer and a roll of paper towels. "Who?"

"The ants."

Mr. Foster ripped a few sheets of towel off the roll. "They're enough to drive you crazy."

"It's not like having rattlesnakes or scorpions in your kitchen," Fiona said reasonably.

He reached back with the paper towels. "Will you dampen these, honey?"

Fiona ran the towels under the faucet and squeezed them out. "The ants might just be passing through." She handed him the wet towels. "Why is it the first thing people think of when they see anything *really* little is to squash it or spray it?"

Mrs. Foster came in the back door. "Fiona, that dog is lying on his back on our front porch, looking like a large dead bug. And if he comes to life and jumps on the mail carrier, we could be sued." Setting a sack on the counter, she took out a can of spray.

"Since there's nothing to eat under the sink, maybe

the ants will get discouraged and leave," Fiona said.

"Why don't we have sandwiches for lunch?" Mrs. Foster asked her husband. "Then we won't have to wash dishes before we spray."

"If we give them a couple of days to leave on their own," Fiona argued, "they might never come back."

Her mother opened a loaf of bread, and her father started taking jars out of the refrigerator.

"Fiona, would you move the dog, and get the dish of water off the steps before somebody steps in it?" Mrs. Foster fished in the pickle jar with a fork.

"You're going to do it, aren't you?" Fiona asked flatly. "You're just going to go ahead and do it, no matter what I say!"

Mr. Foster put his hand on Fiona's cheek and looked down at her sincerely. "Honey, we don't want you to feel bad, but we can't just turn over the house to an ant colony. Now, you go do what your mother asked."

"My parents take me for granted. Even *dogs* take me for granted." Fiona trudged out of the kitchen.

"Poor lamb," she heard her mother murmur. "She *is* in a mood today."

As Fiona came out the front door, Spike clambered to his feet, wagging as if he'd been left alone for weeks. He looked like a haystack in a hurricane, especially since he wagged his whole body, and shed as he wagged.

Fiona untied his leash and led him through the gate to the side yard. After she looped the end of his leash over the knob of the garage door, she went back through the gate to fetch the water dish.

She set it far enough from Spike so he couldn't step in it, then went around to the back door.

On the kitchen table were paper plates and cups and napkins. Even the sandwiches and fruit and pound cake were on paper plates.

Fiona picked up a sandwich and started to peel back the bread.

"*Don't* open it," her mother said. "It's chopped olive."

Fiona piled sandwiches and cake on a paper plate. "I guess I'll eat outside, so I won't have to think about the ants being slaughtered."

"*Good,*" her father said.

"Wait a minute," Mrs. Foster said, as Fiona headed for the door. "You are not to feed chopped olives and pound cake to that dog."

Fiona began putting the sandwiches back slowly, half by half.

With a sigh, Mrs. Foster handed her two other sandwich halves. "That is all he gets. And he'll have to settle for peanut butter." Then she took all but one slice of pound cake off Fiona's plate.

Fiona took time to put an apple in her mouth before she picked up the plate and a cup of lemonade.

With an apple in her mouth and her hands full and

Spike leaping up to greet her, she had to move very, very carefully.

Sitting down a few feet from him, her back against the garage wall, she tossed him half a sandwich.

He gulped it, then sat with his eyes fixed on her plate.

"Boy," she muttered. "Nobody can stare at food the way a dog can." She tossed him the second half of a peanut butter sandwich. "Don't try to make me feel guilty. If you chewed like a normal person, you wouldn't finish so fast."

He watched her eat.

After half a chopped-olive sandwich, she gave up. "Okay." She tossed him the other half sandwich. "Here's the deal. The pound cake is all mine. Howard wouldn't want you to eat it anyway. It's full of sugar."

She turned her back to Spike, and saw what she hadn't noticed when she had been navigating with her hands and mouth full.

A line of ants stretched from the bushes by the fence, across the walk, and into the flower bed under the bathroom window.

Fiona heard the back door open. "I'll spray around the foundation of the house," she heard her father say, "so they don't find another way in."

Fiona leaped to her feet, scattering crumbs.

There is no way to move a line of ants. There is no way to hide a line of ants, or to reason with a line of ants.

Fiona heard the hiss of the spray can.

Spike got to his feet, growling under his breath.

Mr. Foster came around the corner of the house, aiming the spray at the foundation.

"Wait!" Fiona stepped between her father and the ants.

"Move, honey." Her father aimed the nozzle at the wall by his feet and pressed the button.

Barking savagely, straining at the leash, Spike sprang forward.

"What . . ." Mr. Foster pulled Fiona back. "Stay clear!"

"It's the spray can!" Fiona told him. "Spike must think it's a short fat snake."

Spike snarled, his hackles up.

"Burt, you have a phone call from the store. It's some kind of emergency." Mrs. Foster came around the side of the house.

Mr. Foster handed the can to her. "Don't get near that animal!" He hurried around to the back door.

Mrs. Foster ignored Spike, who was wagging like a dust mop being shaken. "I don't know why the store has to have a crisis on your father's day off. Where did he stop spraying?"

"Ma'am?" Fiona tried to look puzzled.

Mr. Foster opened the bathroom window. "I have to run back to the store. The sprinkler system has flooded the optical department and the sprinkler company's answering machine doesn't work. Where are my shoes?"

"Where did you stop spraying?" Mrs. Foster asked him.

"About where you're standing. I can't go to the store in rubber thongs, Mae."

Thongs seemed like sensible footgear to wear to a flood, Fiona thought, but she knew this was no time to say so.

"Look under the bed." Mrs. Foster aimed the spray can at the foundation of the house.

At the first hiss Spike leaped forward, snarling and barking.

"What in the world . . ." Mrs. Foster thrust Fiona behind her.

"Back!" Mr. Foster shouted at Spike through the screen. "Back, I say!"

"Spike's protecting you!" Fiona told her mother. "He thinks the can's attacking you. See? As soon as you stop spraying, he wags his tail."

"That dog's a killer!" Mr. Foster yelled through the window.

"Oh, don't be silly, Burt," Mrs. Foster said. "It *is* the spray can."

"You stay out of his reach anyway," Mr. Foster called to Fiona. "Where under the bed?"

"Wherever you left them," Mrs. Foster said, but she set the spray can on the chimney ledge and walked around to the back door.

Fiona went after her. "Shall I throw away the spray can?" she asked hopefully.

"Don't you touch it!" her mother said firmly. "I'll finish up after the dog's gone."

In all the furor, Fiona's parents hadn't even noticed the line of ants. "But they'll be back," she told Spike. "You won't be here to hold them off forever."

She squatted a few inches clear of him and watched the ants.

They'd discovered a few of the pound cake crumbs on the walk. Two or three were working at each crumb, pushing and hauling, even trying to lift it. Other ants were running back along the line, rubbing feelers with the newcomers excitedly, as if to say, "Hey, guys! You won't believe this! Wait until you see what dropped out of *nowhere!*"

"Look at them," Fiona told Spike. "So happy. So thrilled. No suspicion that they're going to be wiped out."

As she watched, an idea gathered itself together in her mind. The ants were trying to move the crumbs *away* from the house. Carefully, she crawled back along the ant trail, under the scraggly bushes in the side yard. There, by the side fence, was a big sandy anthill.

Fiona heard the station wagon depart.

She hurried around the back of the house to the kitchen.

She could hear her mother working on the computer in her office.

There was no pound cake left. Fiona spooned a little white sugar into a paper cup. It's probably no better for ants than it is for people, she thought, but it beats being sprayed. Then she made up little foil packets of peanut butter, honey, and granola, and put them in the cup.

Fiona hurried out. There was no sense interrupting her mother to explain. There was no point in calling her mother's *attention* to the ants.

As soon as he saw Fiona coming around the house, Spike began yelping and dancing.

More ants were trying to move more pound cake crumbs.

As Fiona crawled under the bushes with the paper cup in her teeth, Spike was suddenly silent, fascinated.

Several inches from the anthill, Fiona sat back on her heels.

There was no time for anything fancy. She scraped peanut butter and honey off the foil, then off her fingers. She dumped granola into a separate little pile. Then she emptied the sugar.

As she backed out from under the bushes, Spike bounded to greet her. She heard something clank on the walk. Then she saw the knob of the garage door roll across the concrete.

Before she could get to her feet, Spike gamboled toward her.

"*No!*" she cried.

His right front paw landed in the water dish.

As the dish tipped, water swept over the pound cake crumbs and the ants on the walk.

"Fiona?" she heard her mother call.

"I'm all right!" she shouted. "I'm fine! No problem!"

Some of the ants had been swept right off the walk. Some struggled to regain their footing. Some wandered, dazed and aimless. Already, the soaked pound cake crumbs were dissolving.

Fiona knew that anybody who'd been a mother for ten years would not rely on her child's assurance that she'd yelled "No!" without a reason. Fiona knew that if her mother came around the house and saw the ants, she'd simply turn the hose on them and wash them off the walk.

There was also the matter of the garage doorknob.

Fiona dropped to her hands and knees and blew gently on the ants, whooshing them off the walk toward the bushes.

Having been a child for ten years, Fiona knew a pulled-out doorknob called for a prompt confession. She picked up the knob and the soggy paper plate. Holding Spike's leash firmly, she led him around the back of the house.

Spike was in no hurry. He had to smell the flowers and wet on the bushes and eat a little grass and throw it up and jump back in alarm from a caterpillar.

Mrs. Foster was opening the back door as Fiona reached it.

"Why is it suddenly so quiet?" she asked. "Didn't your father tell you to stay clear of that dog? And what's that in your hand?"

Fiona held out her hand. "When the knob came off the garage door, the leash came off the knob."

Spike sat back on his haunches and lifted his front paws, like a bear begging for peanuts.

Mrs. Foster backed into a kitchen chair, sat, and put her head in her hands.

"Mama?" Looping the leash around the railing, Fiona hurried into the kitchen. "Mama, are you laughing or crying?"

"I haven't decided." Mrs. Foster rested her elbows on the kitchen table and her chin on her left palm. "Do I blame the dog, or the person who attached his leash to the knob, or her parents for not telling her to take the leash off the knob?" She stood. "I hate to ignore you on a Saturday, Fiona, but I've got a deadline. Just keep the dog in the backyard and don't let him do any more damage."

Fiona led Spike back to the side yard. "We're just lucky she feels guilty about working when I'm around," she told him.

There was not an ant on the walk. Those in the dirt near it were milling around in confusion. Gripping the leash close to Spike's collar, Fiona crawled under the bushes.

The ants had discovered the food she'd left. A few were investigating the honey and peanut butter and granola. The biggest crowd was gathered around the white sugar.

Suddenly, Spike yelped. Tearing the leash from Fiona's hand, he scrambled out from under the bushes.

Fiona had no idea whether he'd been attacked by ants or was having a fit. "It's okay! It's okay!" Hastily, she backed out from under the bushes.

"Hey, boy!"

Spike was on his hind legs, frantically licking Howard's face.

"What are you doing under the bushes?" Barbara asked Fiona.

Fiona stood. "Watching ants."

"*Ants?*" Barbara echoed. "You turn down a trip to the zoo to watch *ants?* We saw lions, and giraffes, and bears, and hippos—"

"Doing what?" Fiona asked.

"What do you mean, doing what?" Barbara asked. "You expect them to be writing poetry or something?"

"I mean, what were they doing?"

"Not much." Howard rubbed his cheek against Spike's muzzle.

"At least it beats watching ants," Barbara said loftily.

"I don't suppose you know that ants have great table manners," Fiona said, "even though they're junk food freaks."

"Come on!" Barbara scoffed.

"I'll show you." Fiona crawled back under the bushes. "Hang on to Spike."

A few inches from the anthill, she sat back on her heels. "See? Right to the sugar."

Even Barbara was impressed. "Wow! Maybe that's why ants are so small."

Fiona and Howard looked at her.

"They're so polite." Howard leaned his elbows on his knees. "All those ants around one pile of sugar without any of them crowding or shoving."

"And look," Fiona said. "They space themselves evenly, like tiny spokes around the center of a wheel."

"I like those guys who already found the sugar rushing around to tell the ones just coming from the nest," Howard said.

"A few of them are tasting . . . what's that stuff?" Barbara asked.

"Honey, and granola, and peanut butter."

"I feel sorry for the ones trying to tell everybody about the granola," Howard said.

Fiona heard her family station wagon pull into the driveway. "Quick! Back out! Get away from the ants!"

"Why? Why?" Howard and Barbara whispered, but they obeyed.

Fiona urged them out the side gate. "Get Spike away from here!"

She went in through the garage and met her father in the driveway. "Hi, Dad." She tried to think of something that would keep his mind off the ants. "How was your flood?"

"Mmmfth." He trudged up the porch steps. She

could tell by his slouch that it would be some time before he'd feel up to spraying anything.

She caught up to Howard and Barbara and Spike at the corner.

"Why did we have to get away from the side yard?" Barbara asked. "And why did we have to get Spike away?"

"I like having him around, since he won't let anybody kill the ants. But when my father sees where he pulled the knob off the door . . ."

"Wait. Wait." Howard stopped walking. "Spike won't let anybody hurt ants?"

Fiona explained about Spike attacking the spray can.

"Wow!" Kneeling, Howard put his arms around Spike. "Just like Lassie!"

"It was a spray can, not a rattler," Barbara pointed out.

Howard looked up at her coldly. "My *dog* didn't know that."

They walked on to the park. Fiona told them about the ants trying to carry crumbs away from the house, about trying to coax them back to their hill, Spike flooding them, her blowing them off the walk, and Spike pulling the knob off the door.

When she finished, Howard said, "Is it okay

if we come over tomorrow to see what's happening?"

"It won't be easy," Fiona said. "So long as I can feed the ants and keep them under the bushes, they're safe. But we can't call attention to them."

Barbara raised her eyebrows. "Your parents are going to crawl under bushes looking for them?"

"No," Fiona said patiently. "But if we're hanging around there all the time, they're going to wonder why."

"One of us can stand watch," Howard suggested. "If I even hear a door open, I'll warn you. It'll be exciting. . . ."

"How come *we* go to the zoo, and everything exciting happens to *you?*" Barbara asked Fiona. "We don't even *get* ants around our house."

"Sure you do," Howard said. "You probably just don't notice unless they get in and everybody starts making a fuss."

This was what Fiona had been trying not to think about. "I couldn't save the ones in the house," she murmured.

Howard stopped and faced her and put his hands on her shoulders. "Hey. Fiona. How many people do you know who could have saved *any* ants? What would happen to those ants in the yard if they didn't have you to count on?"

When Fiona got home, she didn't go back to the kitchen for a snack. She was afraid it would still smell of ant spray.

Hearing the *click click click* of computer keys, she wandered into her mother's office. Mrs. Foster sat squinting at the monitor, her glasses sliding down her nose.

Fiona felt as if somebody put a hand around her heart and squeezed, not hard but tight. I love them so much it hurts sometimes, she thought. They spray ants without even thinking about it. But that's the way they were brought up.

Mrs. Foster swiveled around in her chair. She looked tired and rumpled, but she smiled and put her arms out. "Hi, sweetie!"

Fiona hugged her, wondering what would happen if she told her mother the whole story.

"Want something to eat?" her mother asked, still holding her.

"Could we have it out on the porch?"

Fiona went into the downstairs bathroom and

washed her hands. When she came out, her mother was sitting on the front-porch swing with two bananas and a box of English tea biscuits.

Fiona sat on the swing, peeling the banana her mother had started for her. It was almost four o'clock, the time when the heat of a July day shimmers off the sidewalks, and people go inside—unless they're running through sprinklers with their friends. The street was so quiet, you could hear the murmuring of bugs.

"You're right about being famous." Fiona took a tea biscuit out of the box. "It could be a pain." She remembered what Howard had said. "You know what does feel good, though? What feels really good is being somebody to count on."

"You are one smart kid," her mother said.

It also feels good to be appreciated, Fiona thought. But she was sure any mother already knew that.

Thinking About It

1. Fiona felt it was her responsibility to save the ants from harm. Have you ever felt responsible for someone or something in trouble? Did things work out for you as well as they did for Fiona? Tell about it.

2. Even though Fiona was happy she saved the ants in the yard, she still had her regrets about the final outcome. What did she still feel bad about? What would you tell her to help her feel better?

3. Fiona chose one solution to the problem of the ants. As Fiona's friend, what advice would you offer her about other solutions?

Another Book About Ants
In *Two Bad Ants* by Chris Van Allsburg you can follow a couple of ants on a hair-raising adventure.

URBAN ROOSTS

Where Birds Nest in the City

Written and illustrated by Barbara Bash

Early in the morning you can hear something rustling up on the ledge of an old stone building. Even before the city awakens, the birds are stirring in their urban roosts.

All across the country, as their natural habitats have been destroyed, birds have moved to town. The ones that have been able to adapt are thriving in the heart of the city.

One familiar urban dweller is the pigeon. Long ago it was called a rock dove, because it lived in the rocky cliffs along the coast of Europe. Today it flourishes all over the United States in the nooks and crannies of our cities.

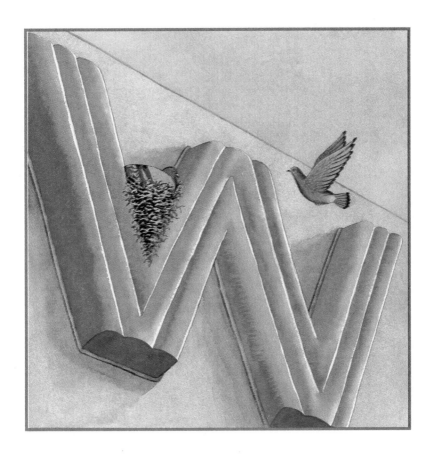

To the pigeon, the city may look like a wilderness full of high cliffs and deep canyons. The cliffs are buildings made of stone and brick and glass, and the canyons are windy avenues full of cars and people. Flying together in flocks, pigeons explore the city canyons looking for food and spots to roost.

A roost is a place where birds go for protection when they sleep and for shelter from the rain and cold. Pigeons roost under highway overpasses, on window ledges, under building archways, on top of roofs, and under eaves. Sometimes their roosts are so well hidden you have to watch carefully to find them.

Look up under the train trestle. Pigeons may be roosting along the dark beams. Watch the open windows of an abandoned building. Hundreds of pigeons could be living inside, flying in and out all day long.

A nest is a place where birds lay their eggs and raise their chicks. Often it's in the same spot as the roost. Pigeons build a flimsy platform of sticks and twigs and debris up on a ledge, or on a windowsill, or in a flowerpot out on a fire escape, or in the curve of a storefront letter.

Throughout the year, pigeons lay eggs and hatch

female

HOUSE
SPARROW

male

male

HOUSE FINCH

female

their young. The female sits quietly on her clutch, and after eighteen days fuzzy chicks begin to appear. Five weeks later, after their adult feathers are fully developed, the young pigeons fly away to find homes of their own.

Sparrows and finches are successful city dwellers, too. Introduced from England in 1870 to control insects, the house sparrow has chosen to live close to people all across the United States. The house finch was originally a West Coast native, but some caged birds were released on the East Coast in 1940, and the species quickly spread. Sparrows and finches don't migrate, so you can watch them at backyard feeders throughout the year, chirping and chattering as they pick up seeds.

The little hollows in and around building ornaments and Gothic sculptures are favorite nesting spots for sparrows and finches. These cavity nesters can slip into the tiniest spaces. Some of their nests are visible and others are completely hidden from view.

In the spring, you may see a small bird flying overhead with a twig in its beak. If you follow its flight, it will lead you to its nest. Watch the bird land and then disappear into a crevice or behind a stone curve. A few moments later it will pop out again, empty-beaked, and fly away to search for more nesting material.

Sparrows and finches can even find spots to nest out in the middle of the busiest intersections. At the top of some streetlights, there's a small opening where the lamp meets the pole. If you look carefully, you may see a tiny house finch slip inside.

Or watch the short open pipe at the top of some traffic light poles. A pair of house sparrows may be darting in and out, bringing food to their nestlings. Sometimes you can even spot a nest in the metal casing that surrounds a traffic light. Perhaps the heat of the bulb helps keep the eggs warm.

A tiled roof can house so many sparrows and finches it looks a little like an apartment complex. All day long the birds bring nesting material and food for their chicks into the small hidden cavities behind the tiles. When the chicks get too big for the nest, they play on top of the tiles, testing their wings before their first flight.

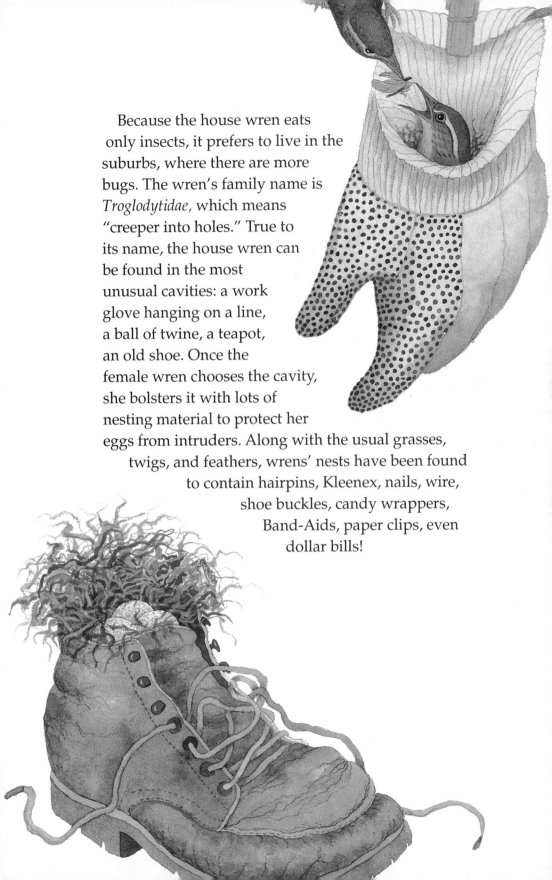

Because the house wren eats only insects, it prefers to live in the suburbs, where there are more bugs. The wren's family name is *Troglodytidae*, which means "creeper into holes." True to its name, the house wren can be found in the most unusual cavities: a work glove hanging on a line, a ball of twine, a teapot, an old shoe. Once the female wren chooses the cavity, she bolsters it with lots of nesting material to protect her eggs from intruders. Along with the usual grasses, twigs, and feathers, wrens' nests have been found to contain hairpins, Kleenex, nails, wire, shoe buckles, candy wrappers, Band-Aids, paper clips, even dollar bills!

The barn owl lives in the city, too, but few people see it because it flies while everyone sleeps. All night long its pale, ghostly form soars over the buildings as it hunts for rats and mice to bring to its young.

The barn owl's eyes can see in the dark and its ears can hear the tiniest scratching. Even its voice is suited to city life; when it cries out in the night, it sounds like brakes screeching.

At daybreak, barn owls return to their nests to
sleep. They like to live under train and highway
overpasses and inside old barns and steeples. Instead
of building nests, they lay their eggs in flat, protected
spots. As baby barn owls grow, they huddle together,
hissing and slurping, as they wait for their parents to
return with food.

The nighthawk is a ground-nesting bird; it looks
for a level open surface on which to lay its eggs.
Because city ground is full of cars and people, the
nighthawk often hatches its young up on flat
graveled rooftops.

If you look up on a warm summer night, you
might see a nighthawk swooping low over the
streetlights, sweeping hundreds of insects into its
large gaping mouth. Or you might hear its call in the
dark . . . *peent* . . . *peent*. . . .

   Like the nighthawk, the killdeer makes no nest.
It lays its eggs out in the open, in spots where the
mottled eggshell pattern will be well camouflaged. In
the city you might find killdeer eggs sitting on the
gravel at the edge of a parking lot or next to a train
track. Once, killdeer eggs were even found along the
end line of a soccer field!

The barn swallow used to nest under the natural
overhangs of cliffs. Now its nest can be found under
the eaves of a house or up in the rafters of a garage.
Often attached to a vertical surface, the nest is a cup
made of mud and clay mixed with straw and grass,
and lined with soft feathers.

In the fall, chimney swifts migrate south in groups. You might see them just before sunset as they circle around and around a large chimney, all flying in the same direction. As the sky deepens, they begin to drop inside, like a long stream of smoke being drawn back down the chimney. Inside, the swifts cluster like shingles on a roof, clinging to the sooty walls with their sharp nails.

During the winter, crows also flock together in large groups. They roost at night in the tops of trees in city parks. At dusk, one or two arrive first, perching on high branches and making a silky rustle with their wings. As the light fades, more crows appear and the clamor increases. They make rattling sounds, catlike cries, and metallic squeaks while they jostle for spots. As the darkness deepens, the calls gradually die down, until only an occasional gurgle is heard. Then the crows settle in for the night.

Winter plumage

Summer

Starlings gather in large groups, too—often roosting all along the ledges of a building. When the winter is coldest, they crowd together in crevices to keep warm. Over a hundred starlings have been found huddled side by side in a cavity only two feet wide and three feet deep.

In November, snowy owls migrate down from the arctic tundra to spend the winter in northern cities. They seem to like the windswept environment of airport landing fields—perhaps because it reminds them of home. The owls roost out on the open ground, blending in with the snowy whiteness.

At dusk the snowy owls begin hunting for mice, rats, and rabbits. They fly slowly and silently, their heads turning from side to side, their eyes scanning

the ground for movement. Sometimes snowy owls
will crouch on a small mound of snow and wait,
completely still, for prey to wander by. The sound of
the jets doesn't seem to faze them at all.

Cars and trucks lumber noisily over big city
bridges. But underneath, hidden among the beams
and girders, peregrine falcons have found a home.
Sleekly built with powerful wings, the falcon is one of
the fastest birds on earth. In the city it soars high

above the bridges and buildings, hunting for pigeons and small birds flying below. When it spots its prey, the falcon folds its wings tight against its body and dives straight down at speeds of over one hundred fifty miles per hour!

In cities all across the country, people are fascinated with the peregrine falcon and are doing what they can to make this noble bird feel welcome. In many cities people set nesting boxes filled with gravel out on skyscraper ledges. The falcons seem to like these windy, rocky heights, for they return to the boxes early each spring to lay their eggs and raise their chicks. Living on these high perches with no natural enemies and plenty of pigeons, the falcons are adapting well to urban life.

So many birds make their homes in the midst of the city—sparrows and finches, barn owls and snowy owls, swallows and swifts, nighthawks and killdeers, pigeons and wrens, crows, starlings, and falcons. Each has found its own urban roost.

Thinking About It

1. You've just read about some of the survivors in nature. Which of them would you like to live with for a while?

2. Why would a writer pick this topic to write about? Why would a reader pick this topic to read about?

3. Suppose Barbara Bash visits your neighborhood. Where would you take her to find some surprises in nature? What might she choose to write about?

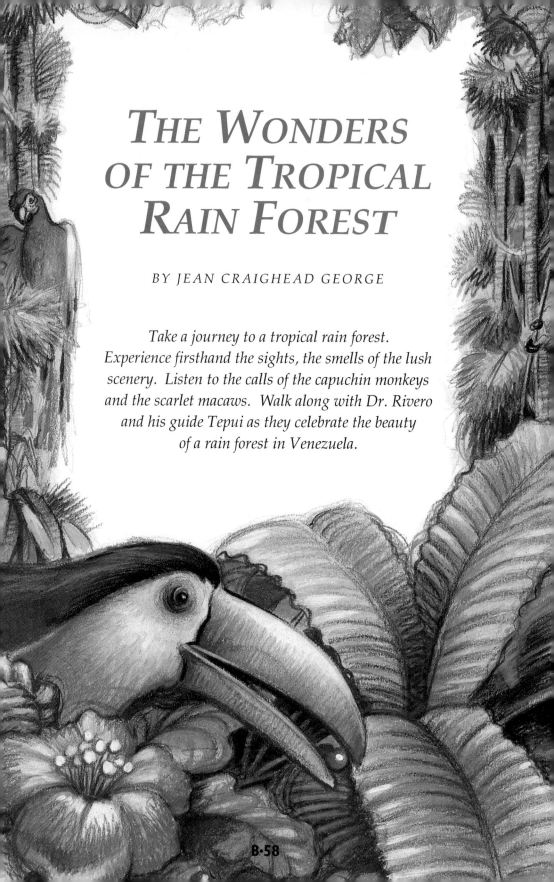

THE WONDERS OF THE TROPICAL RAIN FOREST

BY JEAN CRAIGHEAD GEORGE

*Take a journey to a tropical rain forest.
Experience firsthand the sights, the smells of the lush
scenery. Listen to the calls of the capuchin monkeys
and the scarlet macaws. Walk along with Dr. Rivero
and his guide Tepui as they celebrate the beauty
of a rain forest in Venezuela.*

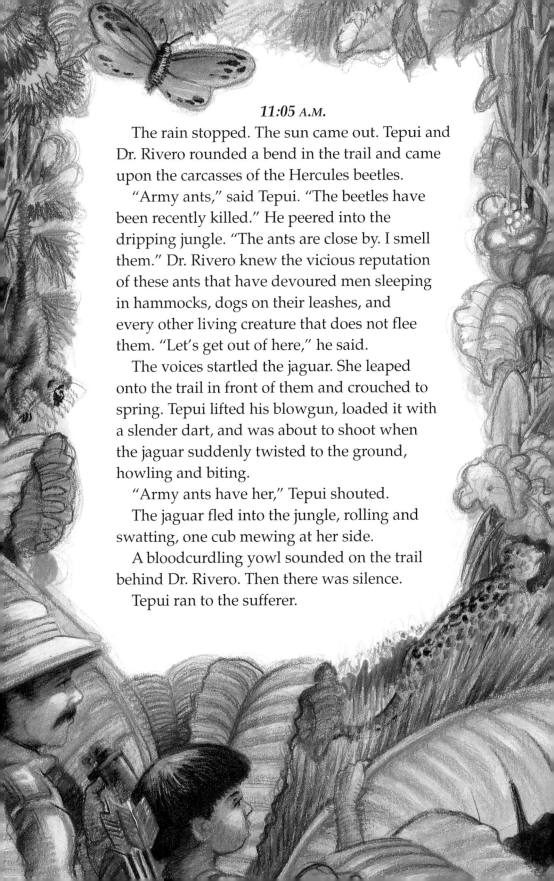

The rain stopped. The sun came out. Tepui and Dr. Rivero rounded a bend in the trail and came upon the carcasses of the Hercules beetles.

"Army ants," said Tepui. "The beetles have been recently killed." He peered into the dripping jungle. "The ants are close by. I smell them." Dr. Rivero knew the vicious reputation of these ants that have devoured men sleeping in hammocks, dogs on their leashes, and every other living creature that does not flee them. "Let's get out of here," he said.

The voices startled the jaguar. She leaped onto the trail in front of them and crouched to spring. Tepui lifted his blowgun, loaded it with a slender dart, and was about to shoot when the jaguar suddenly twisted to the ground, howling and biting.

"Army ants have her," Tepui shouted.

The jaguar fled into the jungle, rolling and swatting, one cub mewing at her side.

A bloodcurdling yowl sounded on the trail behind Dr. Rivero. Then there was silence.

Tepui ran to the sufferer.

11:10 A.M.

"The army ants are killing a beautiful jaguar cub," he lamented as Dr. Rivero joined him. The scientist was still both shaken and awed by the sight of the big angry cat. He wiped perspiration from his brow.

Although Tepui and Dr. Rivero knew the law of the jungle—one dies that another can live—it was difficult to be a witness to this truth. They turned and went on.

"Ouch," yelled Dr. Rivero. "Ants!"

"Run!" said Tepui. "Knock them off as you run. Scatter them. Without each other they are helpless." He broke into a run himself, knocking ants from his ankles.

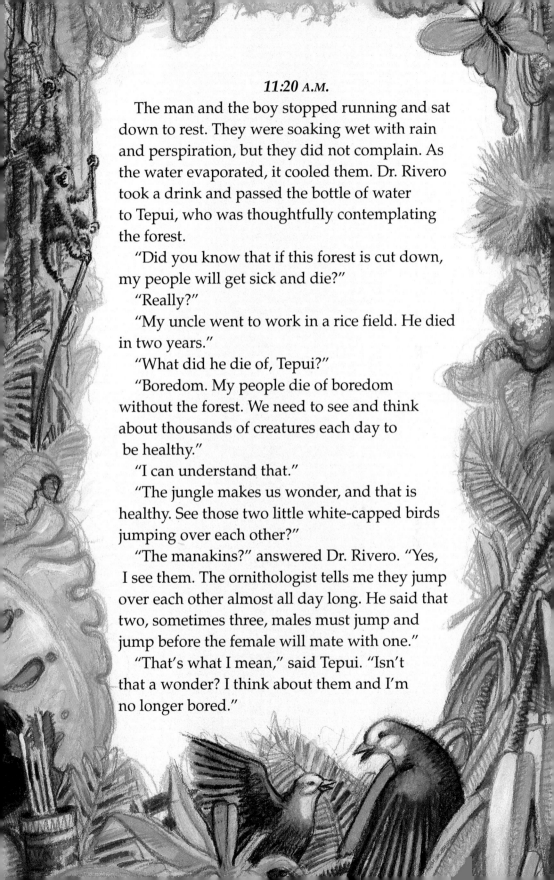

The man and the boy stopped running and sat down to rest. They were soaking wet with rain and perspiration, but they did not complain. As the water evaporated, it cooled them. Dr. Rivero took a drink and passed the bottle of water to Tepui, who was thoughtfully contemplating the forest.

"Did you know that if this forest is cut down, my people will get sick and die?"

"Really?"

"My uncle went to work in a rice field. He died in two years."

"What did he die of, Tepui?"

"Boredom. My people die of boredom without the forest. We need to see and think about thousands of creatures each day to be healthy."

"I can understand that."

"The jungle makes us wonder, and that is healthy. See those two little white-capped birds jumping over each other?"

"The manakins?" answered Dr. Rivero. "Yes, I see them. The ornithologist tells me they jump over each other almost all day long. He said that two, sometimes three, males must jump and jump before the female will mate with one."

"That's what I mean," said Tepui. "Isn't that a wonder? I think about them and I'm no longer bored."

LOOKING AT THE WORLD BENEATH MY FEET

BY JEAN CRAIGHEAD GEORGE

One night my grown son Luke, who is a biologist, held me spellbound as he recounted the mysteries of the rain forest. He was packing his bags to go to Venezuela where his friends, all scientists, were studying the rain forest birds, mammals, plants, insects, amphibians, and fishes. Together they hoped to begin to penetrate the mystery of how each living thing in those tropical forests interacts with all the others to make a whole of many parts. "Want to go along?" he finally asked.

That's all I needed to hear. A month later I awoke in a hammock on the porch of a research station in a tropical rain forest in Venezuela. The dawn and I were greeted by the chime of rain, the call of birds, the howl of monkeys— and the voice of a slender native boy. He was telling Luke about the men on bulldozers who were coming to mow down and burn the trees of his forest home.

When the boy departed, Luke came to me shaking his head. "Wouldn't it be wonderful," he said as he dreamed, "if we could save the forest for that splendid little boy." He then told me that there were many unknown and unnamed creatures in the rain forest. "And," he went on, "there are people who might buy and save a rain forest if we found a creature never before seen by humans and named it for one of them." I looked at him dubiously. "Well, I can dream, can't I?" He smiled.

I thought about Luke's dream for the remainder of my visit. As I learned about the forest and its creatures, I began writing a story in my head. I named the native boy Tepui, the Indian word for the massive one-mile-high mesas of Venezuela. The forest became the Rain Forest of the Macaw after I looked up one morning to see thirty red, blue, and yellow scarlet macaws take off through the jungle like sky rockets. The unknown creature became a butterfly,

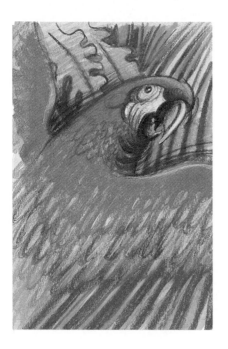

one of many among the millions that glide over and through the forest without a name.

Two months later I was home writing *One Day in the Tropical Rain Forest.*

That is how most of my nature books are born. I share the excitement of learning with the scientists who are studying different environments. Then I make the local children my heroes and, in this case, fulfill Luke's dream by saving the rain forest. If you read the book, you and Tepui will link together macaws, army ants, jaguars, termites, Hercules beetles, birds, trees, flowers, and butterflies minute by minute during one day to create a glorious rain forest for yourself.

Rocking in a hammock is a beautiful way to gather material for a book. Other treks have been more strenuous. Twice I camped on the Arctic ice north of Barrow, Alaska, at 35 below zero. I have climbed mountains and camped in the thin air above alpine tundras, and I have gotten down on my hands and knees and looked at the city within a city— the sidewalk.

I loved writing about a sidewalk. It is a desert. It can be hot, cold, dry, or flooded.

Winds streak across it and tough plants adapt and survive in its cracks and crannies. Its heroes are ants, beetles, spiders, and birds. They are strong, ingenious creatures that can live where few can— all upon a sidewalk. They also make life interesting for folks who get down on all fours and look at the world beneath their feet.

ALL
UPON A
SIDEWALK

BY JEAN CRAIGHEAD GEORGE

The sun came over the curve of the earth, lit up the city, and awakened the wild things on 19th Street.

A sparrow yawned, a cricket chirped, and Lasius flavus peered out of her doorway in a crack in the sidewalk.

She was a yellow ant with big eyes, narrow waist, and a glittering assortment of six spindly legs.

Her apartment-like home lay under the sidewalk. It had corridors, pantries, nurseries, and other rooms. There were barns for the ant cows—little turtle-shaped scale bugs and humped-back aphids.

Every morning Lasius flavus and her sisters carried the cows outside and set them to graze on the stems of the crabgrass that grew in the dust in the crack. In the late afternoon they brought the cows back to their barns, milked them, and fed the food to the queen ant.

Lasius flavus, like all the billions of ants on the earth, was a natural chemist. Tiny laboratories in her abdomen mixed enzymes and acids into mysterious

fluids and gases. In the chemicals were messages that were "heard" by other ants on their elbowed antennae and jointed jaws.

One day the queen said in a chemical message, "We need some sugar." Lasius flavus went out on the sidewalk and gathered sugar from candy and chewing gum wrappers.

When the queen asked for pollen in a different chemical message, Lasius flavus ran under some steps and gathered gold balls from country flowers that had been carried to town and dropped by the wind.

Today, however, Lasius flavus did not know where to go. The queen had asked for a wondrous treasure called Euplectus confluens. It was terribly appealing, and hidden somewhere in the city. Lasius flavus had but one clue—a taste of Euplectus. The queen had acquired it in some food from the sidewalk, but where it had come from the ants did not know.

Lasius flavus climbed out of the crack and scanned

the vast desert before her. The sidewalk, to her, was
pitted with craters; each sand grain was a rock, each
pebble a boulder. The cracks were canyons.

Lasius flavus took to the highway her sisters had
built with layers of chemicals. She found nothing
appealing along its course, just carbon from cars and
oil from the street. She stepped into a groove made
long ago by the sidewalk maker's cement trowel. The
groove was carpeted with a tiny green moss. It grew
from dusty seed spores that floated in the air and
came down to the sidewalk in droplets of rain.

As she walked along, she laid down a chemical
trail of her own so she could find her way back home.

Far down the groove she came to a cave made by a
stone that had been pried out of the cement by the ice
of winter. A spider lurked in it.

The spider had sailed into the cave on a long thread
of silk she had spun from her body after hatching
from her egg. She had flown over the treetops, over

the river, and around the buildings to 19th Street. Reefing in on her sail, she had steered herself to the cave near the ant house. There she was ready to trap ants that came down the groove. An evil chemical poured from the cave, warning Lasius flavus not to go on. She scrambled quickly out of the groove!

A dark cloud loomed on the sidewalk. Lasius flavus pulled down her antennae and lowered her head as a dust storm struck. Pollen from the pines in the park, fungi spores from the wood in old buildings, sand, soot, and dust whirled around her. She tested each scent; but none was appealing.

Climbing up on a bottle cap, she listened with all her six ears that lay like drumheads on the sides of her body. A migrating swallow called from the sky. A mountainous taxi roared down the street.

Lasius flavus turned in another direction. Wings whistled and whined. A fruit bee was coming her way as it languidly cruised above the 19th Street sidewalk.

Lasius flavus stood up on her two back feet, opened her jaws, and picked up the scent from the bee. It was sweet with the juice of a pear it had sipped at the fruit stand.

But it was not *appealing*.

The treasure-seeking Lasius flavus was not even tempted to follow the bee. Instead she climbed down from the bottle cap and walked gingerly out on the huge, endless sidewalk.

Suddenly her hard outer coat tightened against her body. She knew what this meant! The air pressure was dropping, a rain storm was coming. She wheeled on all six feet and hastened her gait.

She zigged toward a building to investigate a rumble. It was only the roots of a wall pepper plant bulldozing into the dust by the building. The plant had sprung from a seed that had been brought to the sidewalk in the droppings of a bird.

Lasius flavus was sipping moisture from a leaf when a whirling propeller smashed into the wall. It was an air-traveling seed from the tree of heaven eight blocks away. It lodged by the wall pepper plant and, absorbing some water, instantly started to build a root. But it was not appealing.

People were passing. Their footfalls made cyclones. Lasius flavus ran into a soda straw.

In a calm she dashed for the curb. A boot slammed to the sidewalk and gusted her under the cellophane wrapper from a cigarette pack. She climbed into it, looking for something appealing, just as a sparrow picked up the wrapper.

The bird lifted Lasius flavus off the sidewalk. He went up in the air past windows and ledges, past layers of bedrooms, up up to the roof of a very tall building. There the bird stuffed the ant and the cellophane into his nest.

Lasius flavus ran out of the cellophane, over the ledge, and straight down the building headfirst. She came to the sidewalk and cricked her antennae. She was far from her trail, out of touch with her home, lost on the strange section of sidewalk.

Quickly Lasius flavus began to circle wider and wider as she looked for her trail. She found a snail egg that had dropped off the toe of a pigeon who had just returned from the riverbank. She found a watch beetle that lives in the wood of doors, windowsills, tables, and benches.

But she did not find her trail!

Desperately she circled this way and that, rounded the corner, and stepped onto the highway of the avenue ants. Lasius flavus spun her antennae, walked on her hind legs, darted and zagged. On *this* highway there was something appealing.

It grew stronger and stronger as she followed the

trail, up a step, up a flowerpot, and into the home of
the avenue ants. The avenue ants lived around the
corner from Lasius flavus in the shade of bright
petunia plants.

Lasius flavus stopped running. A pit lay before her,
the deep dark shaft of an earthworm's home.
Suddenly a mammoth fire engine thundered down
the avenue. The flowerpot rocked. The dry earth
crumbled, and Lasius flavus fell into the pit.

Dirt poured on her head. The worm hole collapsed
and opened a wall into the home of the avenue ants.

In the rubble and debris was something appealing!
Lasius flavus threw back the stones. There in the dust
sat Euplectus confluens, an insect known as the ant-
loving beetle. The treasure was found.

The beetle opened his mouth and stuck out his
tongue. It was broad and exactly fitted the contours
of her face. With a soft lick he said, "Please feed me."

Lasius flavus stuffed him with food from her body. As she did so, the yellow hairs on his back turned into fountains. From them an exotic drink welled up that tasted like flowers and gardens and herbs.

When Lasius flavus had drunk from the fountains, the ant-loving beetle held out his antenna. It was shaped to exactly fit the joints of her mouth. Lasius flavus closed her jaws on the knob and picked up Euplectus as if he were a little frying pan.

The soil rumbled. The avenue ants were coming after her.

They wanted their beetle back! Lasius ran up the worm hole, around the flower stems, and down to the sidewalk. The avenue ants swarmed out of the flowerpot. But Lasius flavus turned off her trail-making chemicals as she rounded the corner. Now there was no way for the other ants to track her. But where was her own trail? She was lost on a prairie of

cement. The wind blew, raindrops splashed and formed little lakes. The lakes joined together and created a sea. Lasius flavus climbed up on a matchstick. The sea became an ocean, the matchstick a boat. Lasius flavus and the ant-loving beetle sailed down the sidewalk.

They rammed into a bottle cap, fell off the matchstick, and were pulled by the current far under the water. They spun into a cave made safe by a bubble of air. But it was also the lair of the spider!

The spider opened her jaws. Two poison fangs rolled out.

Instantly Lasius flavus brewed up a chemical. She laid a foul-smelling wall around herself and the ant-loving beetle. The spider backed up and crawled deep into her cave.

The rain stopped, the ocean sank, and Lasius flavus looked out at the sun. She picked up her treasure and

scampered up the groove. Her highway was gone, washed away by the rain. Using her eyes, she found her way past familiar craters.

Finally she came to the edge of her crack. Her door was not there. It had been crushed by the flood. Lasius flavus drooped her antennae. Her spindly legs collapsed at the joints. She sank to her belly as the ant-loving beetle turned on his fountains—a delicious message went out!

Sand rumbled, dust heaved, and up from the sidewalk came some of her sisters. They pushed up the sand, opened the door, and welcomed the treasure and Lasius home.

THINKING ABOUT IT

1. Lasius flavus has to use all of her strength and intelligence to find the Euplectus confluens. Tell about a time when you had such a challenge.

2. If you were to give Jean Craighead George her next nature assignment, what would you ask her to write about? Why would she be a good writer for the subject you chose?

3. Jean Craighead George helps readers realize that nature is interesting everywhere. What in nature is near to you? How would you show that it is interesting?

Another book by Jean Craighead George

In *One Day in the Prairie* the author proves that the wide open prairie can be just as exciting as a busy city street or a lush, remote jungle.

WHAT A WONDERFUL WORLD

Words and Music by
George David Weiss and Bob Thiele

I see trees of green, red roses too,
I see them bloom for me and you,
and I think to myself
What a wonderful world.

I see skies of blue and clouds of white,
the bright blessed day, the dark sacred night,
and I think to myself
What a wonderful world.

The colors of the rainbow, so pretty in the sky
are also on the faces of people goin' by.

I see friends shakin' hands, sayin', "How do you do!"
They're really sayin' "I love you."
I hear babies cry, I watch them grow
They'll learn much more than I'll ever know
and I think to myself
What a wonderful world.
Yes, I think to myself
What a wonderful world.

Nose High

from TURTLE IN JULY by Marilyn Singer   illustrated by Jerry Pinkney

Barn Owl

February night
        (sweep)
Thick clouds
No moon
        (search sweep)
Soft snow
No ice
        (hush sweep)
Patience
Silence
Wait for the
        (sweep)
        squeak
Now swoop
        snatch
        crack
A hard time for owls
But harder still for mice

March Bear

Who I?
    Where I?
When I now?
    No matter
Need water
Few berries
Fresh ants
    Not so hungry
Or am I?
Don't think so
    Not yet
And anyway it's too early for honey
Funny
That odor
    This river
That hollow
    This den
I know them
    Well, sort of
I've been here
    But when?
    No matter
New morning
Remember it then

Turtle in July

Heavy
Heavy hot
Heavy hot hangs
Thick sticky
Icky
But I lie
Nose high
Cool pool
No fool
A turtle in July

Timber Rattlesnake

Summer it still is
    Yes
September stones
Warm bones
Warm blood
Strike I still can
    Yes
Snare and swallow the harvesting mouse
                  the shuffling rat
But slant they do the sun's rays
Shorter grow the days
    Yes
Soon September stones
Chill bones
Chill blood
Stiff shall I grow
And so below I'll slide
Beneath stones
Beneath soil
Coil I still can
    Yes
Sleep safe
Sleep sound
Snake underground

Beavers in November

This stick   here
That stick   there
    Mud, more mud, add mud, good mud
That stick   here
This stick   there
    Mud, more mud, add mud, good mud
        You pat
        I gnaw
        I pile
        You store
This stick   here
That stick   there
    Mud, more mud, add mud, good mud
        You guard
        I pack
        I dig
        You stack
That stick   here
This stick   there
    Mud, more mud, add mud, good mud
        I trim
        You mold
        To keep
        Out cold
This stick   here
That stick   there
    Mud, more mud, add mud, good mud

NATURE:
A KALEIDOSCOPE OF
WONDER AND SURPRISE

BY JERRY PINKNEY

My first interest in animals and nature came very early in my life. As a child we had pets around the house. I had tropical fish and the care of a rabbit. My grandfather raised chickens. As a result, I became concerned with the treatment of animals.

Years later my wife and I gave our four children a dog. The family named him Two Bits. Over the years we've adopted four cats. I believe the cats sparked another interest in me. I discovered that each cat has quite a different and unique personality. Clorox was the smartest; Brillo, the most playful; Midnight, the most clever; and Shadow, the funniest (especially as a kitten). These differences got my attention. I became even more fascinated with animals and nature.

I have worked on many projects involving the drawing of animals, but *Turtle in July* by Marilyn Singer presented me with the opportunity to zero in on each animal's personality. I was excited about this project. The poems were written so as to give a sense of the attitude and physical qualities of each animal. My challenge was to do paintings of each animal that would reflect, enhance, and give life to the poems. The first step in envisioning an animal is for me to put myself inside of the creature—for me to pretend to be that particular animal. For example, for "March Bear," I thought about the size and the sounds it makes. I thought about how it moves (slowly or quickly), where it lives, what it eats, and so on.

The research comes next. I have a large library of nature

books and magazines. I also keep a scrap file made up of clippings of animals and nature.

When I start a drawing, I get as many pictures of the animal as possible. I begin working on a thumbnail sketch. I am trying at this point to work out the way I will later illustrate the animal. Will it be a close-up or a view from some distance? Most of the illustrations in *Turtle in July* are close-ups. My intent was to have the animals look out at the viewer, as if they were reciting the poems. If you read the poems, especially out loud, you can feel what I wanted to achieve. It was also important to me to have the animal look as natural as possible.

My favorite painting of those shown is the timbersnake because of the texture of its skin and the configuration of the snake's body. I am fascinated with the varied qualities of each animal.

I've always been interested in details in my work. Animals and nature provide me with ample textures and patterns to work with. Look closely at the bark of a tree and the colors in a butterfly's wings. The animal world is a kaleidoscope of wonder and surprise.

Sketch for "March Bear"

B·95

THE
DESERT'S
CHILDREN

from *The Desert Is Theirs*
by Byrd Baylor
illustrated by Peter Parnall

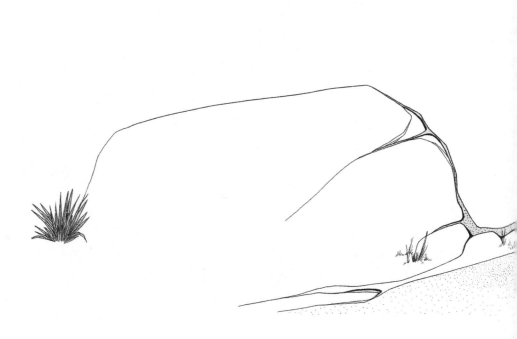

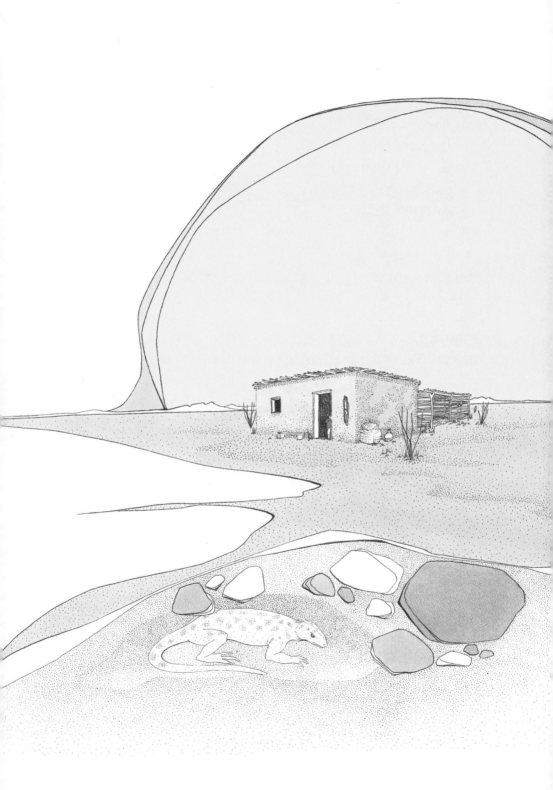

Papagos try
not to anger
their animal brothers.
They don't
step on
a snake's track
in the sand.
They don't disturb
a fox's bones.
They don't shove
a horned toad
out of the path.
They know
the land belongs
to spider and ant
the same as it does
to people.

They never say,
"This is my land
to do with as I please."
They say,
"We share . . .
we only share."

And they *do* share.

A deer likes
the same sweet seeds
and wild berries
that Indian children hunt.

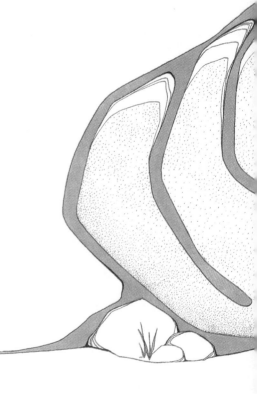

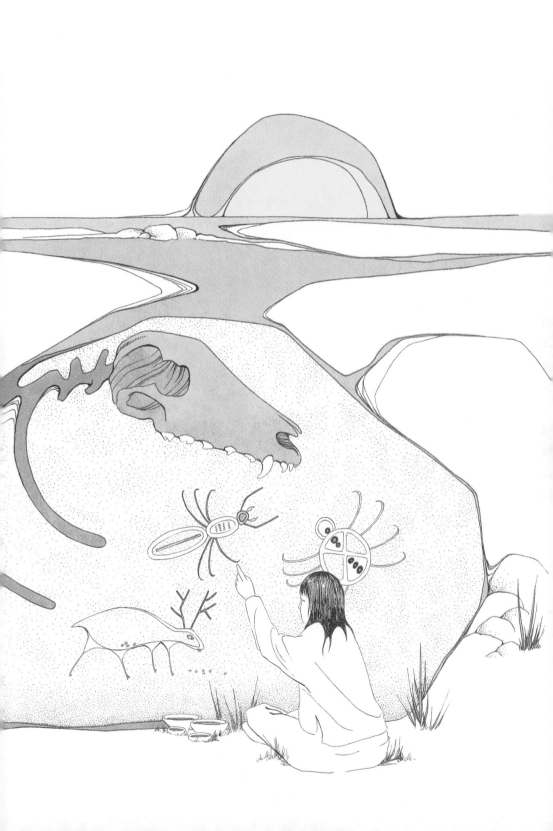

You'll see doves
dipping down
for the
juicy red fruit
that grows high
on a cactus . . .
and you'll see
Indian children
hold out their hands
for the same summer treat.

You'll see pack rats
hiding their treasure,
their good mesquite beans.
But they can't have them all.
People are storing them too.
Pack rats and people both know
to save some for tomorrow—
or later.

The desert gives
what it can
to each of its children.

THINKING ABOUT IT

1. Think of "Nose High" as your invitation to slither with a snake or build a dam with a beaver. What do you see, hear, taste, and feel?

2. In his essay, Jerry Pinkney says that in order to draw an animal he first puts himself inside of the creature and pretends to be that animal. Do you think that works? Why?

3. At the end of her poem, "The Desert's Children," Byrd Baylor writes: "The desert gives/what it can/to each of its children." What would you give to the desert in return?

Another Book About Nature
They may be some of the tiniest creatures on earth, but they can empty a room by simply walking into it. *Someone Saw a Spider: Spider Facts and Folktales* by Shirley Climo explores the world of these fascinating and frightening fellows.

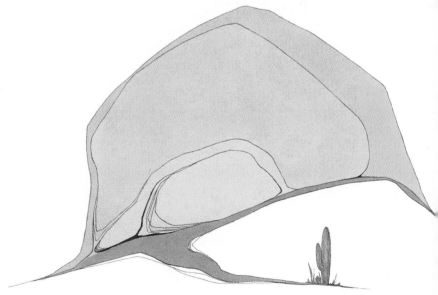

THE GROWIN' OF PAUL BUNYAN

from *A Telling of the Tales*

by William J. Brooke

This is a story about how Paul Bunyan met up with Johnny Appleseed an' what come about because o' that meetin'. But it all got started because o' the problems Paul had with his boots one mornin'.

The hardest thing for ole Paul about gettin' started in the mornin' was puttin' on his boots. It wasn't so much the lacin' up that got him down (although when your bootlaces are exactly 8,621 feet an' four an' three quarters inches long, an' each one has to be special ordered from the Suwanee Steamship Cable Company in New York City, an' if because you're strong as ole Paul you tend to snap about two laces a week as a rule, then just tyin' your boots can be a bit of an irritation, too).

No, the hardest part o' puttin' on his boots was makin' sure he was the only one in 'em. Because, you see, they was so big an' warm that all the critters liked to homestead in 'em. So he'd have to shake 'em for nine or ten minutes just to get out the ordinary rattlesnakes an' polecats. Then he'd reach in an' feel around real careful for mountain lions an' wolf packs an' the occasional caribou migration. Fin'ly he'd wave his hand around real good to see if any hawks or eagles was huntin' game down around the instep. Then he could start the chore o' lacin'.

But ever' now an' then, no matter how careful he was, he'd miss a critter or two an' then he'd just have to put up with it. 'Cause once he had those laces all done up, it just wasn't worth the trouble to untie 'em all again.

So on this partic'lar day ole Paul is out o' sorts because of a moose that's got stuck down betwixt his toes. Paul's appetite is so spoiled he can't get down more than three hunnert pancakes an' about two an' a half hogs worth o' bacon afore he grabs up his ax an' takes off to soothe his ragged nerves in his usual way by shavin' a forest or two.

Well, the more his toes itch, the faster he chops; an' the faster he chops, the more his toes itch. Fin'ly, he can't stand it no more, so he sets down on a medium-size mountain an' undoes all 8,621 feet, four an' three quarters inches o' his right bootlace an' takes it off an' shakes it out for twenty minutes afore he remembers it was his left foot that was itchin'. So he gives a big sigh an' starts in on the other boot.

Fin'ly, both boots is off an' a slightly bruised moose is shakin' his head an' blinkin' his eyes an' staggerin' off betwixt the stumps. An' Paul has his first chance to take a deep breath an' have a look round. An' he's surprised, 'cause he can't see any trees anywheres, only stumps. So he gets up on a stump an' looks around an' he still can't see any standin' timber. He'd been so wrought up, he'd cleared all the way to the southern edge o' the big woods without noticin'.

Now this annoys Paul, 'cause he's too far from camp to get back for lunch, an' nothin' upsets him like missin' grub. An' when he's upset, the only thing to soothe him is choppin' trees, an' all the trees is down so that annoys him even worse.

There he sits, feelin' worse by the minute, with his stomach growlin' like a thunderstorm brewin' in the distance. An' then he notices somethin' way off at the horizon, out in the middle o' them dusty brown plains. All of a sudden there's somethin' green. As he watches, that green starts to spread in a line right across the middle of all that brown.

Now the only thing I ever heard tell of that was bigger than ole Paul hisself was ole Paul's curiosity. It was even bigger than his appetite. So quick as he can get his boots on, he's off to see what's happenin'. What he sees makes him stop dead in his tracks. 'Cause it's trees, apple trees growin' where nothin' but dirt ever growed before. A whole line of apple trees stretchin' in both directions as far as you can see.

It makes him feel so good he just has to take up his ax an' start choppin'. An' the more he chops, the better he feels. An' as he marches westward through all the flyin' splinters an' leaves an' applesauce, he sees that the trees is gettin' shorter until they're just saplin's, then green shoots, then just bare earth.

Paul stops short then an' leans on his ax handle to study the funny little man who turns around an' looks up at him. He's barefoot an' wears a gunnysack for clothes with a metal pot on his head for a hat. He looks up at Paul for a second, then he reaches in a big bulgy bag hangin' at his side an' takes out somethin' teeny-tiny, which he sticks in the ground. He gathers the dusty brown dirt around it an' pats it down. He stands up, an' out of a canvas waterbag he pours a little bit o' water on the spot. Then he just stands an' watches.

For a few seconds nothin' happens, then the tiniest littlest point o' green pokes out o' the dust an' sort o' twists around like it's lookin' for somethin'. All at once, it just stretches itself toward the sky an' pulls a saplin' up after it. An' it begins to branch an' to fill out an' its smooth green skin turns rough an' dark an' oozes sap. The branches creak an' groan an' stretch like a sleeper just wakin' up. Buds leaf out an' turn their damp green faces to the sun. An' the apples change from green to red an' swell like balloons full to bustin' with sweet cider.

The funny little man looks up an' smiles an' says, "My name's John Chapman, but folks call me Johnny Appleseed."

"Pleased to meet you," says Paul.

The little man points at his tree. "Mighty pretty sight, don't you think?"

"Sure is," says Paul, an' with a quick-as-a-wink flick o' his ax, he lays the tree out full length on the ground. "My name's Paul Bunyan."

The little man lifts his tin pot an' wipes his bald head while he stares at the tree lyin' there in the dirt. Then he squints up at Paul an' kneels down an' puts another seed in the ground. Paul smiles down at him while the tree grows up, then he lays it out by the first. The little man pops three seeds into the ground fast as can be. Paul lets 'em come up, then he lops all three with one easy stroke, backhand.

"You sure make 'em come up fast," says Paul, admirin'-like.

"It's a sort o' gift I was born with," says Johnny Appleseed. He looks at the five trees lyin' together. "You sure make 'em come down fast."

"It's a talent," says Paul, real humble. "I have to practice a lot."

They stand quiet awhile with Paul leanin' easy on his ax an' Johnny lookin' back along the line o' fallen trees to the horizon. He lifts his tin pot again an' rubs even harder at his head. Then he looks up at Paul an' says, "It seems like we got somethin' of a philosophical difference here."

Paul considers that. "We both like trees," he says, real friendly.

"Yep," Johnny nods, "but I like 'em vertical an' you like 'em horizontal."

Paul agrees, but says he doesn't mind a man who holds a differin' opinion from his own, 'cause that's what makes America great. Johnny says, "Course you don't mind, 'cause when my opinion has finished differin' an' the dust settles, the trees is in the position you prefer. Anybody likes a fight that he always wins."

Paul allows he's sorry that Johnny's upset. "But loggin's what I do, an' a man's gotta do what he does. Besides, without my choppin' lumber, you couldn't build houses or stoke fires or pick your teeth."

"I don't live in a house an' I don't build fires an' when I want to clean my teeth I just eat an apple. Tell me, when all the trees are gone, what'll you cut down then?"

Paul laughs. "Why, there'll always be trees. Are you crazy or somethin'?"

"Yep," says Johnny, "crazy to be wastin' time an' lung power on you. I got to be off. I'm headin' for the Pacific Ocean an' I got a lot o' work to do on the way. So why don't you head north an' I'll head west an' our paths won't cross till they meet somewheres in China."

Paul feels a little hurt at this, but he starts off north, then stops to watch as Johnny takes off at a run, tossin' the seed out in front o' him, pressin' it down into the ground with his bare toes an' tricklin' a little water behind, all without breakin' stride. In a minute he's vanished at the head o' his long line of apple trees.

Now Paul has figured that Johnny hadn't really meant to offend him, but it was more in the nature of a challenge. An' Paul loves any kind of a challenge. So he sets down an' waits three days, figurin' he should give a fair head start to Johnny, who's a couple hunnert feet shorter'n he is. Then at dawn on the fourth day, he stands up an' stretches an' holds his ax out level a foot above the ground. When he starts to run, the trees drop down in a row as neat as the cross ties on a railroad line. In fact, when it came time to build the transcontinental railroad, they just laid the iron rails down on that long line o' apple trees an' saved theirselves many thousands o' dollars.

Anyways, Paul runs for two days an' two nights, an' when the sun's settin' on the third day, he sees water up ahead. There's Johnny Appleseed plantin' a last tree, then sittin' on a high bare bluff lookin' out over the Pacific Ocean. Paul finishes the last o' the trees an' swings the ax over his head with a whoop an' brings it down on the dirt, buryin' its head in the soil an' accident'ly creatin' the San Andreas Fault. He mops his brow an' sits down beside Johnny with his feet danglin' way down into the ocean.

Starin' out at the orange sun, Johnny asks, "Are they all gone?" Paul looks back over his shoulder an' allows as how they are. Paul waits for Johnny to say somethin' else, but he just keeps starin', so Paul says, "It took you six days to plant 'em an' it took me only three days to chop 'em down. Pretty good, huh?"

Johnny looks up an' smiles sadly. "It's always easier to chop somethin' down than to make it grow." Then he goes back to starin'.

Now that rankles Paul. When he beats somebody fair an' square, he expects that someone to admit it like a man. "What's so hard about growin' a tree anyway?" he grumps. "You just stick it in the ground an' the seed does all the work."

Johnny reaches way down in the bottom o' his bag an' holds out a seed. "It's the last one," he says. "All the rest o' my dreams is so much kindlin' wood, so why don't you take this an' see if it's so easy to make it grow."

Paul hems an' haws, but he sees as how he has to make good on his word. So he takes the little bitty seed an' pushes it down in the ground with the tip o' one fingernail. He pats the soil around it real nice, like he seen Johnny do. Then he sits down to wait as the sun sets.

"I'm not as fast as you at this," Paul says, "but you've had more practice. An' I'm sure my tree will be just as good as any o' yours."

"Not if it dies o' thirst," says Johnny's voice out o' the dark.

Paul hasn't thought about that. So when the moon comes up, he heads back to a stream he passed about two hunnert miles back. But he don't have nothin' to carry water in, so he scoops up a double handful an' runs as fast as he can with the water slippin' betwixt his fingers. When he gets back, he's got about two drops left.

"Guess I'll have to get more water," he says, a mite winded.

"Don't matter," says Johnny's voice, "if the rabbits get the seed."

An' there in the moonlight, Paul sees all the little cottontails hoppin' around an' scratchin' at the ground. Not wishin' to hurt any of 'em, he picks 'em up, one at a time, an' moves 'em away, but they keep hoppin' back. So, seein' as how he still needs water, he grabs 'em all up an' runs back to the stream, sets the rabbits down, grabs up the water, runs back, flicks two more drops on the spot, pushes away the new batch o' rabbits movin' in, an' tries to catch his breath.

"Just a little more water an' a few less rabbits an' it'll be fine," Paul says between gasps.

Out o' the dark comes Johnny's voice. "Don't matter, if the frost gets it."

Paul feels the cold ground an' he feels the moisture freezin' on his hands. So he gets down on his knees an' he folds his hands around that little spot o' dirt an', gentle as he can, breathes his warm breath onto that tiny little seed. Time passes and the rabbits gather round to enjoy the warmth an' scratch their soft little backs up against those big callused hands. As the night wears on, Paul falls into a sleep, but his hands never stop cuppin' that little bit o' life.

Sometime long after moonset, the voice o' Johnny Appleseed comes driftin' soft out o' the dark an' says, "Nothin's enough if you don't care enough."

Paul wakes up with the sun. He sets up an' stretches an' for a minute he can't remember where he is. Then he looks down an' he gives a whoop. 'Cause he sees a little tiny bit o' green pokin' up through the grains o' dirt. "Hey, Johnny," he yells, "look at this!" But Johnny Appleseed is gone, slipped away in the night. Paul is upset for a minute, then he realizes he don't need to brag to anybody, that that little

slip o' green is all the happiness he needs right now.

As the sun rises, he fetches more water an' shoos away the crows an' shields that shoot from the heat o' the sun. It grows taller an' straighter an' puts out buds an' unfurls its leaves. Paul carries in all the animals from the surroundin' countryside, coyotes an' sidewinders an' Gila monsters, an' sets 'em down in a circle to admire his tree growin' tall an' sturdy an' green.

Then Paul notices somethin'. He gets down on his hands an' knees an' looks close. It's a brown leaf. "That's not too serious," he thinks an' he shades it from the sun. Then he sees another brown leaf an' he runs back to get more water. When he gets back, the little saplin' is droopin' an' shrivelin'. He gets down an' breathes on it, but as he watches, the leaves drop off an' the twigs snap. "Help me, somebody," he cries out, "help me!" But there's no answer 'cept the rustlin' o' the critters as they slink away from him. An' while he looks down at the only thing he ever give birth to, it curls up an' dies.

For a second he just stands there, then he pounds his fists on the ground an' yells, "Johnny! Johnny! Why didn't you tell me how much it could hurt?"

He sets down an' he stares till the sun begins settin'. Then he jumps up an' says, "Only one thing's gonna make me feel better. I'm gonna cut me some timber! Maybe a whole forest if I can find one!" He reaches for his ax.

An' that's when he sees it. It stretches right up to

the sky, with great green boughs covered with sweet-smellin' needles an' eagles nestin' in its heights. Johnny must have worked some o' his magic afore he left, 'cause when Paul struck it into the ground it wasn't nothin' but an ax. But now, in the light o' the settin' sun, it shines like a crimson column crowned in evergreen.

"I'll call it a redwood," says Paul, who knew now he'd never want an ax again as long as there was such a tree.

So he waited for the cones with the seeds to form an' drop, an' he planted them all over the great Northwest an' nurtured them an' watched a great woodland spring up in their shelter. An' he never felled a tree again as long as he lived.

For years he worked, an' there are those who say you can still catch a glimpse o' him behind the highest mountains in the deepest woods. An' they say he's always smilin' when you see him.

'Cause Paul learned hisself somethin': A little man who chops somethin' down is still just a little man; but there's nobody bigger than a man who learns to grow.

THINKING ABOUT IT

1. How would you read or tell this story
   to make it an important event?
   Demonstrate and give suggestions.

2. In the end, Paul Bunyan comes around
   to Johnny Appleseed's way of thinking.
   What was it that convinced him?

3. Suppose Johnny and Paul visited Tepui
   in the tropical forest. What suggestions
   would they have for each other?

More Stories About the Forest
After you read *How the Forest Grew*
by William Jaspersohn,
you'll wish you could
talk to Paul and Johnny
about it.

Humans:
Friends or Foes?

by Helen Roney Sattler

It was feeding time at the George Sutton Avian Research Center near Bartlesville, Oklahoma. A scientist pulled an eagle-head puppet over her hand and placed a shred of meat in its beak. Then, making as little noise as possible, she pushed the puppet through a small door above the nest of a two-week-old baby Bald Eagle. The eaglet eagerly grabbed the meat and swallowed it.

The scientist is part of a program that is attempting to increase the number of Bald Eagles and to restore nesting populations to former nesting areas throughout the United States. She uses the puppet to prevent direct human contact with the young birds so that they will remain wild.

Bald Eagles in Louisiana and Florida lay eggs from November through January.

If their eggs are destroyed or disappear early during this period, they will lay another clutch (set of eggs). These scientists are taking advantage of this behavior. They remove eggs laid in November, causing the birds to lay a second clutch. The first clutch is taken to the research center and placed in incubators. After they hatch, the eaglets are settled in nestlike tubs located in glass-enclosed, temperature-controlled rooms. When the eaglets are eight weeks old, they are "hacked," or placed in outdoor nests atop wooden towers located in wildlife refuges. For protection, the nests are built inside barred cages. Scientists drop food into the nests every day. The bars are removed from the cages when the eaglets are ready to fly at eleven weeks. The scientists continue to feed the eaglets, however, until

A typical Florida Bald Eagle nest from which whole clutches of eggs are taken.

they are old enough to fend for themselves. It is hoped that the eagles will remain in the area where they are released and establish a nesting territory there when they mature.

This is one of many programs throughout the world that are designed to help prevent the extinction of eagles. In Spain and other places in Europe, scientists remove the second-hatched chicks of Lesser Spotted and Imperial Eagles from their nests. Some are placed in the nests of Black Kites. They are returned to their own nests when the danger of being killed by their nest mates has passed.

Eagles have few enemies besides humans. Natural causes such as disease, severe weather, and starvation when prey is scarce have kept their population in control. Also, animals including crows, raccoons, and snakes eat eggs and eaglets. The number of eagles remained about the same for centuries. In the twentieth century their numbers began to decrease. There are now less than half as many eagles in the world as there were one hundred years ago. Many species are in grave danger of disappearing completely. Some eagles are already so rare that it is extremely unusual to see one.

Humans are to blame for

this. By moving into wilderness areas, cutting trees, and clearing the land, they have destroyed the habitats of many eagles. Some species of eagle adapt to the presence of humans, but most don't. Most will not nest or hunt in areas occupied by humans.

Many countries are trying to protect eagles. In the United States, millions of acres of land have been set aside as sanctuaries for Bald Eagles and Golden Eagles. In Ethiopia, eucalyptus trees have been planted on grassy, treeless plateaus to provide nesting places for Tawny Eagles. Other countries have begun similar projects, but more needs to be done.

Another man-made problem for eagles is contaminated food. Farmers use poisons to kill insects and weeds. Factories spew chemicals that pollute air

A Bald Eagle hatching from an egg. It takes about forty-eight hours for an eaglet to break free of the shell.

and water. Small animals and fish absorb the poisons. When eagles eat the contaminated animals and fish, they too are poisoned. Eagles have died of lead poisoning after eating ducks wounded with lead pellets from hunters' shotguns. Some have been poisoned by bait set for coyotes and other animals. Many countries have passed laws to control pollution and the use of poisons. DDT, an insecticide that causes

A young eagle awaits his breakfast. Special precautions are taken to prevent eagles from too much human contact. Here a puppet is used to trick the eagle into believing he is being fed by his mother.

they believed the birds killed their lambs. Actually, eagles eat very few lambs, and most of those are dead when the eagles find them. Although eagles provide a very valuable service to farmers by killing millions of rodents, sportsmen once shot them because they occasionally killed game birds. Today, many places throughout the world have laws against shooting an eagle. In the United States, the first offense of harming a Bald or Golden Eagle or disturbing the nests, eggs, or eaglets can result in a fine of up to $5,000 or one year in prison.

eagles' eggshells to become so thin they break in the nest, has been banned for most uses in the United States since 1970. However, DDT can last in the environment for over twenty years. It still occurs in some legal pesticides, and it is still a legal product in many countries of the world.

Sheep farmers throughout the world once shot thousands of eagles because

Accidents kill many eagles. Large eagles often use power-line poles for lookout posts. Many have been electrocuted when their long wings touched two wires at once, completing an electric circuit. Some power companies now put barriers on the most dangerous spots to keep the birds from landing or perching on them. Some companies have also started building nesting platforms on power towers that are located in flat, open country where there is plenty of food, but few trees for nesting.

The United States government grants special licenses to people who care for sick or injured eagles in their homes. Eagles that recover completely are released. An injured eagle that can no longer hunt for prey can be kept for breeding. Eaglets born in captivity are placed in the nests of wild eagles or released by the hacking method. Most adult eagles are enthusiastic parents and readily accept and rear foster chicks. Sometimes unreleasable eagles are brought to schools as part of a program to give children a better understanding of

Each day the eagles return to feed at the hack tower. Fresh food is secretly put out for them before the day begins.

these magnificent birds and their problems.

To ensure the survival of the world's eagles, scientists must learn more about the birds and their needs. This is very interesting work, but it is sometimes dangerous and also expensive. The general public, including many schoolchildren, are assisting by donating money to help finance this research.

Some of the money goes to help pay for banding eaglets. Banding helps

A plastic band with an identification number is wrapped around the leg of each eagle. These bands make it easier for scientists to keep track of the activities of individual eagles.

determine the level of the population.

Studying eagles is difficult because they are hard to track after they begin flying. It is easiest to study them in the nest, but that can be dangerous. A scientist may be attacked by adult eagles while climbing a tall tree or cliff to remove eggs or chicks or to band an eaglet. Scientists who do this kind of work, however, are dedicated and think that what they are learning makes it worth the risks.

We now know the causes of many of the problems that threaten eagles. Most of them were created by humans and can be solved. It is our responsibility to find the solutions. Without man-made threats, eagles can take care of themselves very well. Our skies and our lives would be poorer without the presence of the majestic birds called eagles.

scientists learn where eaglets go after leaving the nest. Biologists fasten numbered bands to the chicks' legs and keep track of them as they grow up. Others strap transmitters to the backs of fledglings and track them with satellites. Using airplanes, scientists also locate and count the number of eagle nests, eggs, and eaglets in a specific area to

Thinking About It

1. The government has a program that permits people to care for sick or injured eagles in their homes. Suppose you had such a project at home. What would it be like?

2. What in this article gives you clues about why people work to save eagles?

3. Eagles are one endangered species; there are others. Which endangered species would you like to help? What could you do?

Another Book About Eagles

Learn more about the particular habits of this fascinating bird by reading Aubrey Lane's *Eagles*.

ISAAC ASIMOV'S FUTUREWORLD: TRAVEL ON EARTH

BY ISAAC ASIMOV

Dr. Asimov was born in Russia in 1920. He moved to the U.S. with his family at age 3. He read his first science fiction story at age 9 and earned his first college degree at 19. The renowned scientist and author wrote more than 320 books before his death in 1992.

NOWADAYS, we are caught in a terrible bind. The automobile is by far the most common and most convenient way of traveling across the face of the earth. People would never give them up. And yet automobiles pollute the air dangerously, produce smog, help give people lung cancer, damage vegetation and animal life by causing acid rain, and so on.

What is to be done? In the future, the fuel burned by automobiles will have to be changed. Gasoline contains nitrogen and sulfur impurities that do the polluting. Gasoline can be purified, and less expensive ways of doing this will be found.

Even so, gasoline is made up of molecules containing carbon dioxide which constantly pours into the atmosphere.

Carbon dioxide absorbs and retains the sun's heat. This warms the earth slightly in a "greenhouse effect," and it may alter the climate very much for the worse.

It is possible, however, to use hydrogen gas as a fuel. Of course, it must be formed in some way that doesn't

AUTOMOBILES OF THE FUTURE MAY GET THEIR POWER FROM THE SUN.

water vapor in the process. Hydrogen-driven cars are being experimented with now.

Another possibility is that cars in the future may be driven by efficient electric batteries. Instead of stopping at a service station to buy gasoline, you will stop to exchange your used-up battery for a fully charged one.

Still another possibility is to line the top of the car with photoelectric cells. On sunny days, this will supply electricity to keep the car going. At night or on cloudy days, batteries or hydrogen gas will be used.

Another problem with automobiles is the overcrowding of the highways.

One way of dealing with this is to have traffic lights computerized. Instead of having them go from red to green to red in fixed time, radar can scan the roads leading into an intersection and decide how long the lights should stay green in

involve burning coal or oil, as that would mean carbon dioxide is still produced. The best way is to have it formed by photoelectric cells that convert sunlight into electricity. The electricity can then be used to break up water molecules to give hydrogen.

Hydrogen is explosive, but not much more so than gasoline. On burning, it produces more energy than the same weight of gasoline does, and the hydrogen is changed back into harmless one direction before moving to the other. Traffic would move much more quickly.

Automobiles are now becoming computerized too, and some have road maps fed into the computer "brain." We can look forward to a future when a car can travel by itself along a path determined by the road map. Its radar equipment will cause it to change lanes safely when necessary, to speed up or slow down or stop altogether at times.

IN THE FUTURE, CARS WILL DRIVE THEMSELVES AND ACCIDENTS WILL ALMOST NEVER HAPPEN.

Highway signs will be designed to be scanned by the automobile so it will know where to go if there is an unexpected detour. Every person in the car would be a passenger; there would be no drivers. Such computerized cars may be much safer than ordinary ones, and automobile accidents might become things of the past.

It may be possible for automobiles to ride on compressed-air jets in the future. This would reduce friction to nearly nothing and produce a faster and much smoother ride. It would also reduce the wear and tear on highways and make it much easier to travel on smaller secondary roads. Such automobiles might be able to cross rivers, since the jets would keep them above the water. This would ease congestion on bridges.

Even more far-out is the thought that there could be high-speed travel, either by automobile or by train, through tunnels running under the earth. If the air in

IN THE FUTURE, PLANES WILL TAKE OFF LIKE HELICOPTERS.

Right now, planes need landing fields; the larger and faster the plane, the longer the airstrip it needs. As a result, airports are becoming very crowded. Trying to get the planes up and down without having them collide is difficult. Helicopters can move up and down vertically and can land in small fields if they have to, but helicopters are slow and rather fragile.

What we may use are Vertical-Takeoff-and-Landing planes. They would use no more space than helicopters, but would move straight up and then level out, into a very fast movement, just as rockets do. There would then be room for many more landing places in an airport, and travel might be safer.

It is also possible that airplanes may come equipped with rocket motors as well as ordinary engines. They can be kicked up into near space a hundred miles high in one place and made to come

these tunnels is pushed out and a vacuum created, and if high-temperature super-conductivity produces a magnetic push that keeps the vehicle from touching the ground, it can move along at the speed of an airplane.

Ships could be jet-assisted. Such jets might lift the ship at least partly out of the water and reduce the drag. Using the same power, a ship could move faster than an ordinary ship would. That would cut down the time of sea-travel and help make it smoother too.

What about airplanes?

down in another. With such rocket planes, no place on earth would be more than an hour or so away from any other.

We may even look into the future and see a time when travel on earth is not as necessary as it is now. Often, people travel not because their bodies really must be shifted from one place to another. They are moving only to deliver information, or to pick up information that exists in another place.

However, more and more, it is possible to move the information at the speed of light with no movement of bodies at all. What's more, people can see at a distance, without having to move to someplace else, and they can also handle controls and direct mechanical devices at a distance.

In the future, people living at home could well view their offices or factories, operate machinery, and consult other people miles and miles away by closed-circuit television.

In general, they could run the world without moving from the spot. Having millions of people travel daily into cities and out of them will become a relic of the dark ages. Commuting will dwindle.

Increasingly there will be travel on earth only for people who want to see old friends and relatives and actually touch them, or who want to see sights of the world. It will be easy for them to do this, for the people who would be crowding along with them on business will be doing that business at home.

AS COMMUNICATION SYSTEMS IMPROVE, TRAVEL MAY BECOME UNNECESSARY.

Pulling It All Together

1

Traveling in the future will be very different from the way it is today. Imagine traveling many miles on a trip twenty years from now. Describe the differences from travel today.

2

Many people work to preserve the beauty of nature. They like their work even though it can be frustrating and difficult. Why do they like it?

3

Many parts of nature would be interesting to study closely. Which would you like to get closer to? Tell your reasons.

Books To Enjoy

THE WHEEL ON THE SCHOOL
by Meindert DeJong
Harper, 1954

Titles don't tell you everything. This one doesn't tell you that this book is about noble school kids in Holland, who struggle to bring back the storks that used to roost on their school building.

OLIVER DIBBS TO THE RESCUE!
by Barbara Steiner
Four Winds, 1985

Ollie's at it again! He's the busy ten-year-old who's always getting involved in animal causes. He's got some wild ideas and he tries them all.

MORE SCIENCE EXPERIMENTS YOU CAN EAT
by Vicki Cobb
Harper, 1979

You don't think of your kitchen as a science lab, but you can turn it into one in a jiffy. Everything you'd need is probably there waiting for you.

THE MIDNIGHT FOX
by Betsy Byars
Viking, 1968

To save a beautiful fox from Uncle Fred's anger, Tom must do the bravest thing he's ever done. That won't be easy because Tom isn't naturally brave.

RIVERKEEPER
by George Ancona
Macmillan, 1990
Imagine a man who is paid to guard a river. You might be surprised at the reasons that make it well worth paying him.

THE CITY KID'S FIELD GUIDE
by Ethan Herberman
Simon & Schuster, 1989
You expect to see pigeons and squirrels on city streets. But how about peregrine falcons that can fly at two hundred miles per hour or a huge black bear? Maybe you'd better find out!

GLOBAL WARMING: ASSESSING THE GREENHOUSE THREAT
by Laurence Pringle
Little, Brown, 1990
The earth is getting warmer and warmer. Will the trend continue? What can be done? Be a person who knows about this important change. You may be able to do something about it.

BIG CATS
by Seymour Simon
Harper, 1991
Cats are cats, big or small, but these cats are a lot bigger than your average house cat. "Here, kitty, kitty. Oops!"

Literary Terms

ALLITERATION

Alliteration means sounds that are repeated at the beginnings of words or within the word. In "Turtle in July," the poet begins with three words all starting with the consonant sound *h* and repeats some of them: "Heavy / Heavy hot / Heavy hot hangs." "Thick sticky / Icky" is another example of alliteration; this time the sound is repeated within each word.

EXPOSITORY NONFICTION

Expository nonfiction gives clear, precise information about people, animals, ideas, or special events. Details in the pictures or illustrations add to this information. *Urban Roosts* and "Humans: Friends or Foes" are both good examples of expository nonfiction. They give information about birds: what they look like, where they live, what they eat.

FREE VERSE

Free verse is poetry that makes use of beautifully descriptive language without the regular rhythm or rhyme we sometimes find in poems. "The Desert's Children" is a good example of free verse. It is written in poetic form and uses language such as: "A deer likes the same sweet seeds and wild berries that Indian children hunt."

IMAGERY

Authors use **imagery** to help the reader experience the way things look, sound, smell, taste, or feel. In *Urban Roosts*, sparrows and finches are described as chirping and chattering. The barn owl is described as a ghostly form with a call like brakes screeching. The imagery helps you imagine what these birds are really like.

ONOMATOPOEIA

Onomatopoeia is the use of words that sound like their meaning. In "Barn Owl," the poet uses the words "squeak," "snatch," and "crack" to add to your understanding of how an owl catches a mouse.

REALISTIC FICTION

Realistic fiction has believable characters who seem like real people. The way they act may remind you of people you know. When the word "modern" appears before "realistic fiction," it simply means that the story takes place now, not in the past. "Count on Fiona" is an example of **modern realistic fiction.** Fiona is a character that you might expect to meet on your way home from school today.

TONE

The **tone** of a piece tells you how the author feels about it. The tone in "Count on Fiona" is sympathetic toward Fiona's loneliness. The author seems to feel sorry for Fiona and lets you know how much she misses her old friends. On the other hand, the tone in *Urban Roosts* is neutral. The author approaches the writing with the simpler goal of pointing out information about birds in the city.

Glossary

Vocabulary from your selections

al ler gic (ə lėr′jik), **1** having an
allergy: *Some people who are
allergic to eggs cannot eat them
without breaking into a rash.* **2** of
or caused by allergy: *Hay fever is
an allergic reaction.* **3** INFORMAL.
having a strong dislike: *She is
allergic to physical exercise. adj.*
—**al ler′gi cal ly,** *adv.*

al ler gy (al′ər jē), an unusual
reaction of body tissue to certain
substances such as particular
kinds of pollen, food, hair, or
cloth. Hay fever, asthma,
headaches, and hives are common
signs of allergy. *n., pl.* **al ler gies.**

an ten na (an ten′ə) **1** one of the
long, slender feelers on the head of
an insect, scorpion, lobster, etc.
2 the aerial of a radio or television
set. *n., pl.* **an ten nae** (an ten′ē)
or **an ten nas** for 1, **an ten nas**
for 2.

antennae of a grasshopper

ap peal (ə pēl′), **1** ask earnestly; ask
for help, sympathy, etc.: *When the
children were in trouble they
appealed to their parents.* **2** a call

for help, sympathy, etc.; earnest
request: *an appeal for forgiveness,
an appeal for money for the poor.*
3 call on some person to decide a
matter in one's favor: *When one of
my parents says "No," I appeal to
the other.* **4** a call on some person
to decide a matter in one's favor:
an appeal for another chance.
5 ask that a case be taken to a
higher court or judge to be heard
again. **6** a request to have a case
heard again before a higher court
or judge. **7** be attractive,
interesting, or enjoyable: *That blue
and red wallpaper appeals to me.*
8 attraction or interest: *Television
has a great appeal for most young
people.* 1,3,5,7 *v.,* 2,4,6,8 *n.*

ap peal ing (ə pē′ling), that appeals.
adj. —**ap peal′ing ly,** *adv.*

bore dom (bôr′dəm), a bored
condition; weariness caused by
dull, tiresome people or events. *n.*

carbon dioxide, a heavy, colorless,
odorless gas, present in the
atmosphere or formed when any
fuel containing carbon is burned.
The air that is breathed out of an
animal's lungs contains carbon
dioxide. Plants absorb it from the
air and use it to make plant tissue.
Carbon dioxide is used in soda
water, in fire extinguishers, etc.

cav i ty (kav′ə tē), **1** hollow place;
hole. Cavities in teeth are caused
by decay. **2** an enclosed space
inside the body: *the abdominal
cavity, n., pl.* **cav i ties.**

chemist

chem ist (kem′ist), **1** an expert in chemistry. **2** BRITISH. druggist. *n.*

chem is try (kem′ə strē), **1** science that deals with the characteristics of elements, the changes that take place when they combine to form substances, and the laws of their behavior under various conditions. **2** the application of this science to a certain subject: *the chemistry of foods. n., pl.* **chem is tries.**

clutch¹ (kluch), **1** a tight grasp; hold: *I lost my clutch on the rope and fell.* **2** grasp tightly: *I clutched the railing to keep my balance.* **3** seize eagerly; snatch: *clutch at an opportunity.* **4** Often, **clutches,** *pl.* **a** a grasping claw, paw, hand, etc.: *The fish wiggled out of the hungry bear's clutches and swam away.* **b** control; power: *That country is in the clutches of a dictator.* **5** device in a machine for transmitting motion from one shaft to another or for disconnecting related moving parts. The clutch in an automobile is used to connect the engine with the transmission or to disconnect it from the transmission. **6** lever or pedal that operates this device. 1,4-6 *n., pl.* **clutch es;** 2,3 *v.*

clutch² (kluch), nest of eggs. *n., pl.* **clutch es.**

com mute (kə myüt′), **1** change (a penalty, obligation, etc.) to a less severe one: *The governor commuted the prisoner's sentence from death to life imprisonment.* **2** travel regularly to and from work by train, bus, automobile, etc. **3** the distance or trip ordinarily traveled by a commuter: *a long commute, an easy commute.* 1,2 *v.,* **com mut ed, com mut ing;** 3 *n.* —**com mut′a ble,** *adj.*

con tam i nate (kən tam′ə nāt), make impure by contact; defile; pollute: *The drinking water had been contaminated by sewage. v.,* **con tam i nat ed, con tam i nat ing.** —**con tam′i na′tor,** *n.*

con tem plate (kon′təm plāt), **1** look at or think about for a long time; study carefully: *I will contemplate your offer. We contemplated the beautiful mountain landscape.* **2** have in mind; consider, intend, or expect: *She is contemplating a trip to Europe.* **3** meditate. *v.,* **con tem plat ed, con tem plat ing.** —**con′tem plat′ing ly,** *adv.* —**con′tem pla′tor,** *n.*

crit ter (krit′ər), DIALECT. creature. *n.*

cur i os i ty (kyu̇r′ē os′ə tē), **1** an eager desire to know: *She satisfied her curiosity about animals by visiting the zoo every week.* **2 a** being too eager to know: *Curiosity got the better of me, and I opened the unmarked box.* **3** a strange, rare, or novel object: *One of the curiosities we saw was a basket made from an armadillo's shell. n., pl.* **cur i os i ties.**

de press (di pres′), **1** make sad or gloomy: *I was depressed by the bad news from home.* **2** press down; lower: *When you play the piano, you depress the keys.* **3** make less active; weaken: *Some medicines depress the action of the heart. v.* —**de press′i ble,** *adj.* —**de press′ing ly,** *adv.*

de vour (di vour′), **1** eat (usually said of animals): *The lion devoured the sheep.* **2** eat like an animal; eat very hungrily: *The hungry girl devoured her dinner.* **3** consume, waste, or destroy: *The raging fire devoured the forest.* **4** take in with eyes or ears in a hungry, greedy way: *He devoured the new book about airplanes.* **5** absorb wholly: *I was devoured by curiosity about my birthday presents. v.*

devour

dis turb (dis tèrb′), **1** destroy the peace, quiet, or rest of: *Heavy truck traffic disturbed the neighborhood all day long.* **2** break in upon with noise or change: *Please don't disturb her while she's studying.* **3** put out of order: *Someone has disturbed my books; I can't find the one I want.* **4** make uneasy; trouble: *He was disturbed to hear of his friend's illness.* **5** inconvenience: *Don't disturb yourself; I can do it. v.* —**dis turb′er,** *n.*

dwin dle (dwin′dl), become smaller and smaller; shrink; diminish: *During the blizzard the campers' supply of food dwindled day by day. v.,* **dwin dled, dwin dling.**

eaves (ēvz), the lower edge of a roof that projects over the side of a building. *n. pl.*

fas ci nate (fas′n āt), **1** attract very strongly; enchant by charming qualities; charm: *She was fascinated by the designs and colors in African art.* **2** hold motionless by strange power or by terror: *Snakes are said to fascinate small birds. v.,* **fas ci nat ed, fas ci nat ing.** —**fas′ci nat′ing ly** *adv.*

fell[1] (fel), past tense of **fall.** *Snow fell last night. v.*

fell[2] (fel), **1** cause to fall; knock down: *The blow felled her to the ground.* **2** cut down (a tree). **3** turn down and stitch one edge of (a seam) over the other. *v.* —**fell′a ble,** *adj.*

fell[3] (fel), **1** extremely bad; cruel; fierce; terrible: *a fell blow.* **2** deadly; destructive: *a fell disease. adj.*

fell[4] (fel), skin or hide of an animal. *n.*

foun da tion (foun dā′shən), **1** part on which the other parts rest for support; base: *the foundation of a house.* **2** basis: *This report has no foundation in fact.* **3** a founding or establishing: *The foundation of the United States began in 1776.* **4** a being founded or established. **5** institution founded and endowed. **6** fund given to support an institution. *n.*

gait (gāt), the kind of steps used in going along; manner of walking or running: *A gallop is one of the gaits of a horse. n.*

gnaw (nô), **1** bite at and wear away: *to gnaw a bone. A mouse has gnawed the cover of this box.* **2** make by biting: *A rat can gnaw a hole through wood.* **3** trouble; harass; torment: *A feeling of guilt gnawed at the prisoner's conscience day and night. v.,* **gnawed** or **gnawn** (nôn), **gnaw ing.** —**gnaw′a ble,** *adj.* —**gnaw′er,** *n.*

gra no la (grə nō′lə), a dry breakfast cereal of rolled oats, flavored with other things such as honey, chopped dried fruit, and nuts. *n.*

gun ny (gun′ē), **1** a strong, coarse fabric made of jute, used for sacks, bags, etc. **2** gunnysack. *n., pl.* **gun nies.** [*Gunny* comes from Hindustani *gōnī.*]

gun ny sack (gun′ē sak′), sack, bag, etc., made of gunny. *n.*

hab i tat (hab′ə tat), place where an animal or plant naturally lives or grows: *The jungle is the habitat of monkeys. n.* [*Habitat* comes from Latin *habitat,* meaning "it inhabits," and can be traced back to *habere,* meaning "to have, hold."]

ho ri zon tal (hôr′ə zon′tl), **1** parallel to the horizon; at right angles to a vertical line. **2** flat; level. **3** a horizontal line, plane, direction, position, etc. 1,2 *adj.,* 3 *n.* —**ho′ri zon′tal ly,** *adv.* —**hor′i zon′tal ness,** *n.*

hy dro gen (hī′drə jən), a colorless, odorless gas that burns easily. Hydrogen is a chemical element that weighs less than any other element. It combines with oxygen to form water and is present in most organic compounds. *n.*

in cu ba tor (ing′kyə bā′tər *or* in′kyə bā′tər), **1** box or chamber

for hatching eggs by keeping them warm and properly supplied with moisture and oxygen. **2** any similar box or chamber. Very small babies and premature babies are sometimes kept for a time in incubators. *n.*

jag uar (jag′wär), a fierce animal much like a leopard, but more heavily built. It lives in forests in tropical America. *n.*

jaguar—about 7 feet (2 meters) long with the tail

ma jes tic (mə jes′tik), of or having majesty; grand; noble; dignified; stately. *adj.* —**ma jes′ti cal ly,** *adv.*

maj es ty (maj′ə stē), **1** royal dignity; stately appearance; nobility: *the majesty of the starry heavens, the great majesty of the Grand Canyon.* **2** supreme power or authority: *Judges uphold the majesty of the law.* **3** **Majesty,** title used in speaking to or of a king, queen, emperor, empress, etc.: *Your Majesty, His Majesty, Her Majesty, n., pl.* **maj es ties.**

nest ling (nest′ling), bird too young to leave the nest. *n.*

nestlings

nur ture (nėr′chər), **1** bring up; care for; foster; rear; train: *They nurtured the child as if she were their own.* **2** a bringing up; rearing; training; education: *The two sisters had received very different nurture, one at home and the other at a convent.* **3** nourish: *nurture resentment.* **4** nourishment. 1,3 *v.*, **nur tured, nur tur ing;** 2,4 *n.*

pa tience (pā′shəns), **1** willingness to put up with waiting, pain, trouble, etc.; calm endurance of anything that annoys, troubles, or hurts: *The cat watched the mouse hole with patience.* **2** long, hard work; steady effort. *n.*

phil o soph i cal (fil′ə sof′ə kəl), **1** of philosophy or philosophers. **2** knowing much about philosophy. **3** devoted to philosophy. **4** wise; calm; reasonable. *adj.*
—**phil′o soph′i cal ly,** *adv.*

phi los o phy (fə los′ə fē), **1** the study of the truth or principles underlying all real knowledge; study of the most general causes and principles of the universe. **2** explanation or theory of the universe, especially the particular explanation or system of a philosopher: *the philosophy of Plato.* **3** system for guiding life. **4** the general principles of a particular subject or field of activity: *the philosophy of history, the army's military philosophy.* **5** a calm and reasonable attitude; accepting things as they are and making the best of them. *n., pl.* **phi los o phies.**

pho to e lec tric (fō′tō i lek′trik), having to do with the electricity or electrical effects produced by the action of light. *adj.*

prin ci ple (prin′sə pəl), **1** a truth that is a foundation for other truths: *the principles of democratic government.* **2** a fundamental belief: *religious principles.* **3** a rule of action or conduct: *I make it a principle to save some money each week.* **4** uprightness; honor: *a person of principle.* **5** a rule of science explaining how things act: *the principle by which a machine works. n.*
on principle, 1 according to a certain principle. **2** for reasons of right conduct.

pur i fy (pyùr′ə fī), **1** make pure: *Filters are used to purify water.* **2** become pure. *v.*, **pur i fied, pur i fy ing.**

roost (rüst), **1** bar, pole, or perch on which birds rest or sleep. **2** sit as birds do on a roost; settle for the night. **3** place for birds to rest or sleep. **4** place to rest or stay in: *a robber's roost in the mountains.* 1,3,4 *n.*, 2 *v.*
come home to roost, come back so as to harm the doer or user; backfire; boomerang.
rule the roost, INFORMAL. be master.

rub ble (rub/əl), **1** rough broken stones, bricks, etc.: *the rubble left by an explosion or an earthquake.* **2** masonry made of this: *The house was built of rubble and plaster. n.*

a hat	i it	oi oil	ch child	ə stands for:
ā age	ī ice	ou out	ng long	a in about
ä far	o hot	u cup	sh she	e in taken
e let	ō open	ů put	th thin	i in pencil
ē equal	ô order	ü rule	ŦH then	o in lemon
ėr term			zh measure	u in circus

sanc tu ar y (sangk/chü er/ē), **1** a sacred place. A church is a sanctuary. **2** part of a church around the altar. **3** place of refuge or protection: *a wildlife sanctuary.* **4** refuge or protection: *The cabin provided sanctuary from the rain. n., pl.* **sanc tu ar ies.**

slaugh ter (slô/tər), **1** the killing of an animal or animals for food; butchering: *the slaughter of a steer, to fatten hogs for slaughter.* **2** brutal killing; much or needless killing: *The battle resulted in a frightful slaughter.* **3** kill an animal or animals for food; butcher: *Millions of cattle are slaughtered every year in the stockyards.* **4** kill brutally; massacre. **1,2** *n.,* **3,4** *v.* —**slaugh/ter er,** *n.*

snare¹ (sner *or* snar), **1** noose for catching small animals and birds: *They made snares to catch rabbits.* **2** catch with a snare: *One day they snared a skunk.* **3** a trap: *Flattery is a snare in which fools are caught.* **4** to trap. **1,3** *n.,* **2,4** *v.,* **snared, snar ing.**

snare² (sner *or* snar), one of the strings of wire or gut stretched across the bottom of a snare drum. *n.*

swoop (swüp), **1** come down with a rush, as a hawk does; sweep rapidly down upon in a sudden attack: *Bats swooped down from the roof of the cave.* **2** a rapid downward sweep; sudden, swift descent or attack: *With one swoop the hawk seized the chicken and flew away.* **3** snatch: *The nurse rushed after the running child and swooped him up in her arms.* **1,3** *v.,* **2** *n.* —**swoop/er,** *n.*

ur ban (ėr/bən), **1** of cities or towns: *an urban district, urban planning.* **2** living in a city or cities: *the urban population, urban dwellers.* **3** characteristic of cities: *urban life. adj.* [*Urban* is from Latin *urbanus,* which comes from *urbs,* meaning "city."]

urban

ver ti cal (vėr/tə kəl), **1** straight up and down; perpendicular to a level surface; upright. **2** a vertical line, plane, direction, position, etc. **1** *adj.,* **2** *n.* —**ver/ti cal ly,** *adv.*

Acknowledgments

Text

Page 7: From *Only Fiona* by Beverly Keller. Copyright © 1988 by Beverly Keller. Reprinted by permission of HarperCollins Publishers.

Page 38: *Urban Roosts: Where Birds Nest in the City* by Barbara Bash. Copyright © 1990 by Barbara Bash, illustrations by Barbara Bash. By permission of Little, Brown and Company.

Page 58: From *One Day in the Tropical Rain Forest* by Jean Craighead George. Copyright © 1990 by Jean Craighead George. Reprinted by permission of HarperCollins Publishers.

Page 62: "Looking at the World Beneath My Feet," by Jean Craighead George. Copyright © 1991 by Jean Craighead George.

Page 66: *All Upon a Sidewalk* by Jean Craighead George. Copyright © 1974 by Jean Craighead George. Reprinted by permission of Curtis Brown Ltd.

Page 80: "What a Wonderful World"; words and music by George David Weiss and Bob Thiele. Copyright © 1967 by Range Road Music Inc. and Quartet Music Inc. All rights administered by The Herald Square Music Company. International copyright secured. All rights reserved. Used by permission.

Page 82: From *Turtle in July* by Marilyn Singer, illustrations by Jerry Pinkney. Text copyright © 1989 by Marilyn Singer. Illustrations copyright © 1989 by Jerry Pinkney. Reprinted by permission of Macmillan Publishing Company.

Page 92: "Nature: A Kaleidoscope of Wonder and Surprise," by Jerry Pinkney. Copyright © 1991 by Jerry Pinkney.

Page 96: From *The Desert Is Theirs* by Byrd Baylor. Illustrations by Peter Parnall. Text copyright © 1975 by Byrd Baylor. Illustrations copyright © 1975 by Peter Parnall. Reprinted with permission of Charles Scribner's Sons, an imprint of Macmillan Publishing Company.

Page 102: "The Growin' of Paul Bunyan" from *A Telling of the Tales* by William J. Brooke. Copyright © 1990 by William J. Brooke. Reprinted by permission of HarperCollins Publishers.

Page 118: From *The Book of Eagles* by Helen Roney Sattler. Copyright © 1989 by Helen Roney Sattler. Reprinted by permission of Lothrop, Lee & Shepard Books, a division of William Morrow and Company, Inc.

Page 126: "Isaac Asimov's Futureworld: Travel on Earth" from *Boys' Life*, October 1990. Reprinted by permission of Isaac Asimov.

Artists

Illustrations owned and copyrighted by the illustrator.

Pat Dypol, 6–37
Barbara Bash, 38–57
Malcolm Farley, 58–61, 64, 65
Dave Albers, 66–79
Jerry Pinkney, 83–95
Peter Parnall, 96–101
Jeff Lauwers, 102, 106, 111, 114, 117
Linda Reilly, 127–131

Freelance Photography

Pages 80–81: Michael Goss
Photographs not listed were shot by ScottForesman.

Photographs

Front cover: Ants courtesy of Bruce Coleman Inc.
Front cover, page 2: Toucan courtesy of Loren McIntyre
Page 1: Courtesy Anthro-Photo
Page 3: Ant courtesy of E. R. Degginger/Bruce Coleman Inc.
Page 3: Black leopard courtesy of John Chillman
Page 62: Courtesy Jean Craighead George
Page 92: Photo of Jerry Pinkney courtesy of Myles Pinkney
Page 118: Courtesy Stephen Fettig/GMSARC
Page 120: Courtesy M. A. Jenkins/GMSARC
Page 121–123, 125: Courtesy Sheryl Tatom/GMSARC
Page 124: Courtesy ODWC/GMSARC
Page 132: Courtesy NASA
Page 138: Courtesy Turtox/Cambosco-MacMillan Science Company, Chicago
Page 140: Courtesy Stephen J. Krasemann/DRK Photo
Page 141: Courtesy Tom McHugh/Photo Researchers
Page 142: Courtesy Billy E. Barnes/Stock Boston
Back cover: Fern courtesy of Don and Pat Valenti; Earth courtesy of NASA

Glossary

The contents of the Glossary entries in this book have been adapted from *Intermediate Dictionary*, Copyright © 1988 Scott, Foresman and Company; and *Advanced Dictionary*, Copyright © 1988 Scott, Foresman and Company.